WITH

Frontier Texas
History of a Borderland to 1880

Frontier Texas
History of a Borderland to 1880

Robert F. Pace
and
Donald S. Frazier

State House
Press
McMurry University
Abilene, Texas

Library of Congress Cataloging-in-Publication Data

Pace, Robert F.
    Frontier Texas : history of a borderland to 1880 /
    Robert F. Pace and Donald S. Frazier.
    p. cm.
    ISBN 1-880510-83-9 (hardcover : alk. paper)
    1. Frontier and pioneer life--Texas. 2. Texas--History--
18th century. 3. Texas--History--19th century. 4. Texas--Social
life and customs. 5. Land settlement--Texas--History.
6. Fortification--Texas--History. 7. Indians of North America--
Texas--History. 8. Ranch life--Texas--History. 9. Cattle trade--
Texas--History. 10. Cattle drives--Texas--History. I. Frazier,
Donald S. (Donald Shaw), 1965- II. Title.
    F386.P215 2004
    976.4'02--dc22

                   2004001195

Contents

Maps

Photographs and Illustrations

Preface

Frontier Texas, a technologically sophisticated visitor center and historical attraction, opened in 2004 on the east side of downtown Abilene. It is the expression of a long-cherished vision: a place that would tell the world the compelling story of this fascinating region. This companion book is designed to be a lively narrative—a good yarn—that will inspire readers to further study of the topics encountered in Frontier Texas and further explore our special part of creation. Frontier Texas is also a masterpiece of Abilene community leader H.C. Zachry and bears the indelible mark of his flair for dramatic storytelling, sincere promotion, and civic pride. Thanks to him, the story of the Texas frontier will be told for generations to come.

This book was truly a team effort. Glenn Dromgoole of State House Press was a thoughtful editor whose enthusiasm made writing this book a pleasure, and his eye for deadlines made it a reality. His assistant, Carly Kahl, a talented editor herself, was also instrumental in acquiring illustrations for the book; we are also indebted to readers Robert P. Wettemann, Jr., and Alicia Wyatt, our friends and colleagues at McMurry University, for their excellent suggestions. Finally, and most importantly, none of these efforts would have been possible without our families' unfaltering support—thank you Jill and Catherine, and Susan, Kay, and Sarah. We promise not to write a book next Christmas.

Robert F. Pace and Donald S. Frazier
Abilene, Texas
January 2004

Introduction
The Texas Frontier Borderland

In December 1864, George W. Todd, his wife Dizenia, their fourteen-year-old daughter Alice, and a black slave girl left their home near Spice Rock four miles south of Mason headed to town for church, a routine horseback trip in familiar surroundings. Jym Sloan, an early historian of the region, described the day as "airish," and fresh, a beautiful day for a ride, especially on a good horse like Mrs. Todd's bay racing mare. As the serene party made their way, Mrs. Todd lightened the miles by singing hymns. The road wound its way from their farmstead, along the edge of an oak-choked ravine, and around the base of a conical hill, Todd Mountain, named in true pioneer fashion for the family who first dared claim a home in its shadow. In early Texas, though, there was a price to be paid for this geographic immortality.

As the party rounded the base of their mountain, a band of Comanches—who undoubtedly had a name, now forgotten, for that very same summit—attacked. The first volley of bullets and arrows struck down the servant girl. Although Todd tried to fend off the assault, he was unable to protect his wife and child. Dizenia, whose horse bolted, fell from her mount mortally wounded; the Comanches kidnapped Alice and made their escape. Although Todd and his neighbors

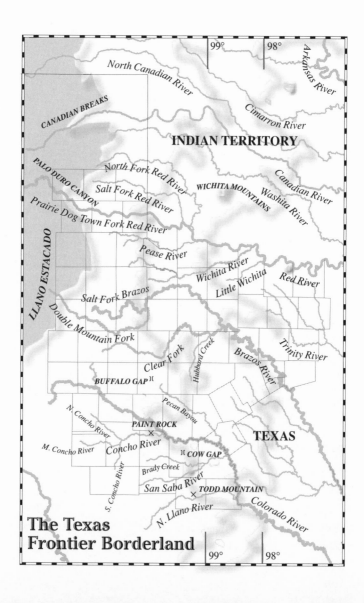

The Texas Frontier Borderland

searched the surrounding region for months trying to find the girl, she was never heard from again.

The story of her capture spread quickly among the settlers in the region, but the news also found an audience among traveling bands of Comanches at an obscure location now known as Paint Rock. Nestled in an outcropping of seventy-foot tall limestone cliffs two hundred feet north of the Concho River in present-day Concho County, this site is the location of nearly 1,500 Indian pictographs stretching more than a half mile. In the days after Alice Todd's capture, perhaps even as he passed that sacred place making good his escape to his home near the Caprock, a Comanche artist told the story of this event in a painting on those cliffs. The pictograph includes two crossed lances to represent an armed conflict, two long-haired scalps to depict the deaths of Dizenia Todd and the slave girl, and a horizontal figure portraying the captivity of Alice Todd. This new tableau, set amid the etchings and flourishes of centuries of Indian artists who felt the power of this place, became another layer of history upon an already ancient land.

In this one episode, the stories of the Texas frontier converge. West Texas has been a crossroads of humanity for thousands of years. Each group of humans who have trekked across its sun-drenched prairies has had to contend with the challenges of life in an area that has always been a climatic, geographical, political, and cultural borderland. In addressing these challenges, the people of the frontier have also had to develop perseverance, toughness, and determination—all necessities for life on the Texas frontier.

Photograph courtesy of Fred and Kay Campbell, Paint Rock, Texas

Pictograph in Paint Rock, Texas of the capture of Alice Todd; includes two crossed lances representing an armed conflict, two long-haired scalps depicting the deaths of Dizenia Todd and a slave girl, and a horizontal figure portraying the captive Alice Todd.

The area encompassing the region stretching from Fort Worth to the Caprock, from Palo Duro Canyon to the San Saba River—with Abilene as its epicenter—was and remains a frontier borderland. The climate changes along this transitional zone. While it shares some of the features of the wetter, more humid eastern climes, it is tempered by the more arid lands to the west. Historian Walter Prescott Webb, in his monumental book *The Great Plains*, identified the 98th to 99th meridians, in degrees west longitude, as the line of "semi-aridity." Beyond this invisible line, trees gave way to grasslands, traditional ways of pioneering would wither before the oppressive sun, and wind made a mournful howl that seemed to dare hardier souls to cross this imagined line in the sand. "It seems to me that this bit of West Texas," wrote A.C. Greene in *A Personal Country*, "is thrown out as a hint or a warning to the traveler that he is approaching another kind of Texas from where he has been . . . unlike the rest of the state in landscape, in people, and philosophy. It is a land for which the stranger should not be unprepared."

Far back into the misty annals of humankind, this precarious threat of calamity was as much real as imagined. Life was cheap, and only the bold and better survived. When *Homo sapiens* first drifted across this stretch of earth, they lived a Hobbesian life that was indeed "solitary, poor, nasty, brutish and short." Even as these ancestors stalked wild animals, teeth and claws turned them into prey as well. It was not enough to outsmart a mammoth. For a successful hunt, one also needed to outsmart the saber-toothed cat. These men and women were not at the top of the food chain or in domination of nature. Instead, they were desperate participants in both—sometimes victors, sometimes vanquished, sometimes banquet.

Water was key. Where it exists, life thrives. Where it does not, it dies. West of this imaginary but potent line, the quest for water determined the quality of life. Traveling was planned with the next spring in mind. Knowledge of the seasonal reliability of creeks and rivers was power. Life was limited by the distance a man could walk to water. The amount he and his family could carry proved a cruel corollary to the equation of time and distance. The endurance of the human body defined transportation on the prairie.

The agricultural revolution that supported the advancement of human civilization never took root in such a land. The balmy and well-watered stretches of Meso-America and the Mississippi Valley gave rise to great towns, boundless fields, and creative populations. These peoples began to develop a sense of wealth. Before long, labor patterns evolved that created a leisure class of nobles and priests, scholars and princes, each of whom lived off of the industry of their neighbors. A classical age emerged that was monumental—literally—in scale. Pyramids and mounds rose skyward as an increasingly sophisticated system of measurements of time, distance, and weight informed these humans of their place in the universe. These great trophies of their civilization were testament to their ability to shape their environment to meet their needs. They had beaten nature. They were its rulers.

But the prairies of western Texas were the asylums of the indigent. Wealth here might mean a bundle of wild pecans, or perhaps an especially hardy pair of moccasins. Here, everyone worked or they starved. These were hunters and gatherers indeed. As these wanderers crossed the prairies, herds of buffalo—estimated to number between ten and twenty million animals—kept maddeningly out of spear and atl-atl range. Always, too, there lurked the packs of gray wolves lingering to set their jaws upon the old, the young, and the weak.

Primitives of an intellectual bent might study the seasons and stars. As was the case with their more affluent distant

Courtesy of Buffalo Gap Historic Village, Buffalo Gap, Texas

Painting depicting an Indian Buffalo Surround

kinsmen, these early marvelers believed that the cosmos held clues to the mystery of the human condition. Even so, among these nomads such observations had at their root a practical purpose. As the sun made its predictable march across the brassy sky, it signaled the cycles of nature that brought game and frost, drought and harvest.

Climate and the creator had conspired to make this place a great dividing line between cultures. To the east, maize ripened in tended fields while families gamboled in their grass and wooden lodges. Common men hunted for food and status while the wisest among them conducted magnificent projects that proclaimed greatness. West of the line, life remained precarious.

Among the first of the distinct groups of humans to claim the region as its own were the Jumanos. Their arrival is hidden in the mists of time, but this Indian group clearly thrived as buffalo hunters and traders and would play a significant role as liaison between the Spanish settlements to the south and other Indian tribes. Sometimes referred to by Spaniards as "naked" Indians because the Jumano women did not cover their breasts, the most striking cultural characteristic was their practice of scarring and tattooing their faces with horizontal lines.

The Jumanos lived a nomadic life. They used skin tepees and hunted with bow and arrow. Because of the large range they traveled—from the northern stretches of the Trinity River in Texas, to the hills of New Mexico, and down to the Rio Grande Valley—the Jumanos participated in widespread trade. They obtained horses early in their dealings with Spaniards and they were instrumental in introducing their usage to other Texas tribes. It was they, by best guess, who first cherished the luxurious campsite at Paint Rock and recorded their minds on its ledges.

The Jumanos disappeared as a distinctive group in the region by 1700 in what remains something of a historical mystery. One thing is clear, however. This decline was accelerated by the emergence of another group into the plains—the Apaches. Another nomadic, buffalo-hunting group, the Apaches waged successful war on the Jumanos for much of the seventeenth century. Some Jumano groups melded into Apache bands, while others took refuge with allies to the east.

Still others, from among the horse-herding Jumanos from the Nueces region, perhaps became the nucleus of the Kiowa Indians, who would rise to distinction on the prairies of West Texas in the next century.

So the ages passed. Conflict defined this hard life on the Texas frontier. The Jumanos, once supreme, disappeared forever like Alice Todd. Their Apache conquerors enjoyed their spoils for a season, feasting on the pecans and buffalo of the Concho valley and painting their version of life on the stony crags. Unbeknownst to them, these newcomers were but a middle link in a lengthening chain and, like their predecessors, the Apache's peace would come to an end at the hands of others seeking their fortunes in this borderland region. By the middle of the eighteenth century, certainly by July 4, 1776, a date more momentous that any of the players then suspected, the struggle over these Texas plains became dominated by two new groups—the Spaniards and the Comanches.

Chapter One
Comanches, Spaniards, and the Land, 1700-1821

What the indigenous peoples of the Texas frontier did not know was that there were other men coming. These bearded, pale-skinned fellows had also, like the denizens of the plains, become wise and had tangled with nature. Driven by a biblical exhortation that gave them dominion over creation, these conquerors had made servants of wind, earth, water, and fire. Starting in 1492 an additional line of human lineage—Spaniards—brought their powerful knowledge to a new world and ushered in a second age.

Yet, despite all of their learning, western Texas defied them. These ironclad men arrived from the south in 1540 to gaze upon a thirsty sea of grass. Despite their best efforts, they never glimpsed a promising future, and their legendary vision failed. The people they encountered, the Indians of the plains, were wretched and poor. Months and years of wandering and exploration revealed no new worlds worth having and these European adventurers left the land and its people alone. Nature, it seems, had won this round and repelled the invader. After a century of neglect, the Spanish returned, but only to the Rio Grande and a string of oases carved out of a region they called "Nuevo Mexico." Another hundred years would

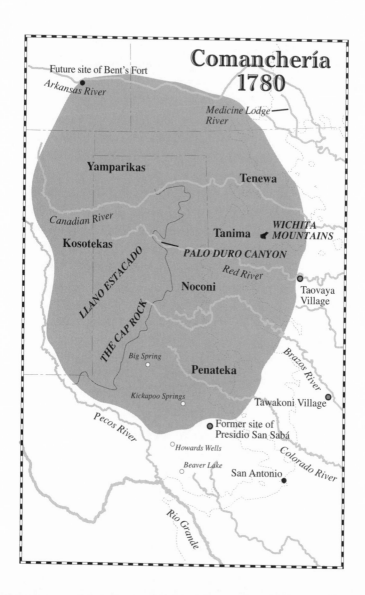

Comanchería
1780

Future site of Bent's Fort
Arkansas River

Medicine Lodge River

Yamparikas

Tenewa

Canadian River

Tanima

WICHITA MOUNTAINS

Kosotekas

PALO DURO CANYON

LLANO ESTACADO

Red River

Noconi

Taovaya Village

THE CAP ROCK

Big Spring

Penateka

Brazos River

Kickapoo Springs

Tawakoni Village

Pecos River

Former site of Presidio San Sabá

Howards Wells

Colorado River

Beaver Lake

San Antonio

Rio Grande

pass before they settled its eastern counterpart—Tejas. The only traces left behind were the occasional relic and Spanish names—Colorado, Brazos—sprinkled upon their maps.

There were other reminders, too. Painted upon the stones at Paint Rock were images of men in black robes and their houses and towers surmounted by crosses. An Indian artist even painted a figure—a man—with horns and a pointed tail, an imported concept of Satan.

Even though they were only occasional visitors and seldom residents of West Texas, the Spanish legacy would be far-reaching. Like a hurricane born off the coast of Africa that carves its path across the Gulf of Mexico, the arrival of these people had, in the words of one historian, created a "storm brewed in other men's worlds." Their microbes devastated Indian populations, and their guns allowed the people of the plains to kill each other with greater efficiency. Even so, these two elements would have had little impact upon this region by themselves. Here, the birthing sound of this new age was a horse's whinny.

The Comanches

The two great constants of this region—time and distance—crumbled beneath horse hooves that ushered in a new age of power and conquest. The geography of West Texas contracted, and success and failure for a people now depended upon their access to horses. Before long new invaders came to western Texas, this time equipped with a combination of both old and new world wisdom. Astride their Spanish ponies, these new horsemen drove every competitor before them. Calling themselves *numuhudu*, or The People, they became what historian Rupert Richardson termed "the Lords of the South Plains." Before long the imagined boundary between wet and dry, verdant and arid, became just as significant as a human border. Western Texas had become *Comanchería*, the domain of the Comanches.

Although the various groups of Comanches shared common cultural characteristics, there was no overall political tribal organization. Historians and anthropologists argue for the existence of between three and twenty major bands of the Comanches from 1706 to 1875. This range of opinions is probably due to the fact that kinship groups and local bands often changed their affiliations depending on various circumstances, including internal discord, disease, warfare, and lack of game. Thus, a group identified one year might evolve into another group a few years later, might join with another band, or might disappear altogether.

Even so, six major bands emerged as being the most important in the history of the Comanches. The Yamparikas ("Yap eaters") inhabited the region between the Canadian and Arkansas rivers, while the Kosotekas ("Buffalo eaters") ranged the Texas Panhandle and eastern New Mexico. The Noconis ("Those who turn back") lived in the Caprock Canyons, the Llano Estacado, and the headwaters region of the Brazos, while the Tenewa ("Those who stay downstream") and the Tanima ("Liver eaters") inhabited the Wichita Mountains and present-day western Oklahoma. The southernmost of the principal bands of the Comanche people, the Penateka ("Honey eaters"), spread out from the Red River southward to the Texas Hill Country. Their usual camping sites were along the banks of the San Saba, Colorado, and Concho rivers as well as the Clear Fork, Double Mountain Fork, and Salt forks of the Brazos River. A seventh band, the Quahadis ("Antelopes"), coalesced in the nineteenth century as fragments and refugees from the Comanches' constant warfare with Texas formed into a belligerent and irreconcilable division of their own.

These erstwhile Shoshones ventured onto the plains in small groups of extended families and relatives known as *numunahkahni*. One or more such groups comprised a local band which the Spanish referred to as *rancherias*. The various rancherias might combine to form villages and bands. Individual *numunahkanis* might move independent of each other, for a variety of reasons, between various bands. Thus, an extended family group long associated with the Noconi might migrate and associate themselves with their distant kin among the Yamparikas.

Over the years, these clans and families ventured south from their mountain homes in search of trade, buffalo, and horses. Once they entered the plains, pressure from the Blackfoot and Crow nations hastened their migration. Arriving on the southern Great Plains in the 1770s, the Comanches dominated a large expanse of land from the Pecos to the Trinity, and the Arkansas to the San Saba. Their raids, however, knew no such bounds.

The size and composition of Comanche local bands were constantly changing. The leader of these groups was a *paraibo*, or what the Spanish referred to as a *Capitancillo*, or "Little Captain." Shedding their Shoshone identity, the Comanches earned their new name from a Ute word for "anyone who wants to fight me all the time" but never numbered more than eight thousand individuals.

Rank, honor, and prestige were the most important factors in most Comanche lives. A male's standing in the tribe came from his individual *puha*, or "medicine power," that he received through the *puhahabitu*, or vision quest. This in turn fostered his aggressiveness in battle, earning still more prestige. "As his deeds increase in daring, he gains a degree of respect from his fellows and visibly takes on authority," wrote a white observer of the Comanches, "little by little, the public confidence in him grows." Men and women both earned respect through acts of generosity. The ultimate honor, though, was to be recognized as a *paraibo*, or principal person of the band. Another person of importance was the *tlatolero*, or camp crier, who helped articulate the decisions of the *paraibo* and his advisors.

The Comanche way of life remained consistently nomadic. Their travels focused on following the migrating buffalo. These beasts provided the Comanches with food, shelter, and clothing. Even though the Comanche diet was predominantly meat, they also supplemented buffalo with fruit, nuts, and wild roots. Occasionally, Comanche bands got produce from neighboring agricultural tribes—primarily the

Wichita and Caddo groups to the east and the Pueblos to the west. The buffalo also provided shelter in the form of tepees—tanned buffalo hides stretched over sixteen to eighteen lodge poles. Finally, Comanche clothing consisted of tanned bison hides or buckskin, formed into breechcloths for men, and fringed skirts, blouses, and leggings for women. Both genders wore tanned hide leggings and moccasins. In winter, Comanches also used buffalo robes to fend off the chill of the frontier weather.

The most notable aspect of Comanche life on the plains, however, was their use of the horse. Comanche children learned to ride at an early age, and horsemanship was an important measure of respect within the Comanche bands. Both men and women reached a level of equestrian skill unmatched anywhere else on the frontier. The horse allowed them rapid mobility in following the buffalo herds and in conducting warfare. Because of this mobility, the Comanches were adept traders who controlled much of the commerce on the Great Plains. They successfully traded horses, captives, and buffalo by-products for a variety of manufactured goods and food.

Comanche political organization had strong democratic elements. A Civil (or peace) chief headed each band, but he was also joined in power by a war chief for times of conflict. Mutual assent within the tribe chose these leaders based on abilities and accomplishments. Chiefs maintained their power only as long as they had the continued support and confidence of the members of their band. Decisions at the tribal level came from a council of chiefs, presided over by a respected head civil chief. Because of the significant level of individual freedom within the tribe, however, individual Comanches were not bound to abide by the decisions of the council, causing many problems in relations with European cultures.

Comanche migration into North Texas began around the beginning of the eighteenth century. This movement brought them into immediate conflict with the Apaches, who had come to dominate the South Plains over the previous century. The two tribes became mortal enemies, as the Apaches had to flee south in the face of the Comanche onslaught. The first documentation of the Comanche presence came in 1743, when a Comanche scouting party entered San Antonio in search of Lipan Apaches. Although there were no hostilities from the encounter, it was clear that the Comanches believed that the Spanish and Apaches were in alliance. This first contact between Comanches and Spaniards ended peacefully, but that would not be the case in the years to come.

Presidio San Sabá

The Spanish in San Antonio found themselves in a dilemma related to the Apaches. These Indians had been the principal irritant to Spanish missions on the frontier because of their constant raids on horse and cattle herds. On the other hand, the Apaches claimed to want a mission of their own. Spanish clergy, therefore, exerted pressure against a military solution to the problem, since the Apaches, they argued, showed some capacity for redemption.

The Spanish finally decided to grant the Apache wish, authorizing the building of a mission on the banks of the San Saba River, to be accompanied by the construction of a *presidio* to house a military garrison nearby. In April 1757 missionaries set out from San Antonio, but conflicts between clergy and the military ensued immediately. The *presidio* commandant and seasoned veteran of decades of plains warfare, Col. Diego Ortiz Parilla, urged the abandonment of the proposed mission because of the uncertain strategic position on the plains. The missionaries, however, prevailed, and construction of both the mission and the *presidio* began in May 1757. The conflict between the military and clergy brought one consequence in construction that would have calamitous consequences: they built the Presidio San Luis de las Amarillas on the north side of the river, seven miles away from the Santa Cruz de San Sabá Mission on the south side of the river.

Within a year, disaster struck. Apache neophytes warned the priests at the mission that "Los Norteños," their enemies from the North, were going to attack. But when Colonel Parilla offered the missionaries and their staff shelter at the *presidio*, he was ignored. On March 16, 1758, two thousand Comanches, Wichitas, and allies launched a surprise assault on the mission, setting fire to the buildings and slaughtering eight of its inhabitants, including two priests. Parilla, whose garrison only numbered about thirty men, sent a detail to the mission after dark to rescue survivors. They saved twenty-seven church workers and volunteers, and shepherded another three hundred civilians from farms along the San Saba back to the *pre-*

sidio. The Comanches left without further incident.

A year and a half later, Parilla led a punitive expedition against Los Norteños to reassert Spanish power and to restore prestige. Nearly six hundred men, including presidial troops from South Texas and Northern Mexico, militia, Indian auxiliaries, and two cannon, left San Antonio in August 1759, crossed the San Saba at the *pre-*

Photograph by R.W. Parvin; Courtesy of the Texas Historical Commission

Ruins of Menard's Spanish fort, Presidio San Sabá

sidio, the Concho at Paint Rock, and moved through what would later become known as Buffalo Gap into the heart of uncharted territory. Near the Clear Fork of the Brazos, Spanish Indian allies overran an unsuspecting Tonkawa camp, killing fifty-five of its inhabitants and capturing more than one hundred. The prisoners told of larger villages, full of much guiltier Indians, to the north and east, and the expedition pushed on.

The invasion did not end well. In early October, Parilla and his army spied a fortified village of the Taovaya Wichitas on the Red River near the site of present Spanish Fort in Montague County. The Spanish troops attacked on October 7, but the Indians, a coalition of various bands, put up a stout defense of the pallisaded town and counter-attacked, capturing the Spanish artillery. Parilla, perhaps the most seasoned and famous Indians fighter on the Spanish *frontera*, ordered a retreat. Once back in San Antonio, he was replaced as commander of San Luis de las Amarillas and forwarded to Mexico City to report on his defeat.

The following year, the new commander on the banks of the San Saba, Filipe de Rábago y Terán, ordered the timber buildings of the *presidio* to be replaced with a more permanent stone construction. The new buildings rose to form a quadrangle fort with four corner bastions. The soldiers also dug a moat to surround the entire site, securing the location for a long Spanish military presence in the region.

The level of permanence afforded by this move was fleeting. Comanches kept constant pressure on the *presidio*, and by 1768 the Spanish position was clearly indefensible. Rábago y Terán ordered his men to withdraw south to the Nueces, abandoning the *presidio* in what turned out to be a permanent move. In 1772 a royal decree officially declared the fort abandoned. The age of the Comanche dominance of the West Texas frontier had come.

Pedro Vial and the Comanches

By the mid-eighteenth century, the Comanches had proven their strength on the Texas frontier. With the loss of the presidio on the San Saba, Spanish officials came to believe that they lacked the military resources to defeat them. As a result, the Spaniards began to pursue peace with the Comanches. The new policy promoted friendship through the use of gifts and trade, and it allowed military force only as reprisals for specific acts of aggression. This policy would remain in effect for the rest of the period in which the Spanish ruled in Texas. The first success of the new approach came in 1762, when Fray José Calahorra y Sáenz got the Comanches to sign a treaty agreeing not to make war against missionized Apaches.

Over the next ten years the Apaches tried to take advantage of the lack of aggression against them and go on the offensive. They attacked Comanche bands and maintained an increasing level of aggression against them, leading the Comanches to go back on their earlier agreement. In 1772 the Spanish then proposed a Comanche-Spanish alliance to eliminate the Apaches. The Comanche chief Povea signed a treaty in San Antonio committing his band to peace with the Spaniards. Other bands, however, continued their raids on Spanish settlements. By the 1780s, Comanche attacks on Spaniards increased sharply, leading Spanish officials to fear that the province of Texas might have to be written off altogether.

In a last-ditch effort to avoid losing Texas, the Spanish government ordered Governor Domingo Cabello y Robles to try once more to negotiate a peace with the Comanches. He wanted to send the right emissary to complete the job, and in a strange twist of history, he chose a Frenchman—Pedro Vial.

Born in Lyons, France, Pierre (Pedro) Vial was an insatiable adventurer. Prior to the American Revolution, he had already explored the area along the Missouri River. In 1779 he appeared in Natchitoches and New Orleans in the Louisiana Territory, an area transferred from French ownership to Spanish sixteen years before. Vial finally made his way to San Antonio after spending some time living among the Taovaya Indians, a group known to associate with the Comanches. It was this connection that caught the attention of Governor Cabello y Robles.

The governor dispatched Vial and Francisco Xavier de Chaves to the frontier with gifts and plans for peace. They spent the summer of 1785 among the Comanches near present-day Baird and Throckmorton, and then returned to San Antonio with three principal Comanche chiefs authorized to make peace with the Spanish. The native chiefs signed the Spanish-Comanche Treaty of 1785, bringing relative peace between the two cultures for the rest of the century.

Vial's success so impressed Cabello y Robles that the governor commissioned him to find the most direct route between San Antonio and Santa Fe. Choosing only one travel companion, Cristóbal de los Santos, Vial set out on October 4, 1786. Shortly after departure, Vial fell ill and became disoriented. He pushed on in a northward direction, arriving at the Tawakoni villages near present-day Waco. From there, the travelers passed through present-day Callahan County and then through the Palo Duro Canyon. They finally found the Red and Canadian Rivers and followed them westward until finally arriving at Santa Fe on May 26, 1787. Instead of finding the most direct route, as ordered, Vial had actually covered around a thousand miles in his circuitous travels.

There were other Spaniards, too, who navigated the Comanche plains. José Mares, a middle-aged soldier from the garrison at Santa Fe, read Vial's travel journals and determined that a more direct and efficient route lay between the capital of New Mexico and San Antonio. On July 21, 1787, Mares, de los Santos, and Alejandro Martín, a native interpreter, made the trek via Palo Duro Canyon to the Taovaya village on the Red River. From there, the party headed south by southwest until reaching San Antonio on October 8. Three months later, he reversed the trip, passing by the abandoned *presidio* on the San Sabá, along the upper reaches of the Colorado, and across the Llano Estacado. He covered more than 1,800 miles in the round trip.

Vial logged many more miles in later years, and long distances clearly did not deter the Frenchman. In 1788 he set out again to establish a route from Santa Fe to Natchitoches. He trekked through the Texas Panhandle, and then once again through what is today Callahan County. Once Vial reached Natchitoches, he set off almost immediately back to San Antonio. And then he returned to Santa Fe, following the route he had established the previous year. By the time Vial reached that western city, he had traveled more that 2,300 miles in fourteen months.

Vial continued his adventurous ways for the next several years. He traveled the round trip of what would later become known as the Santa Fe Trail between Santa Fe and St. Louis, an impressive 2,279 miles. He also gathered significant information about the lives and customs of more than seven major Indian nations. In 1798, he left Spanish service to live among the Comanches, but the next year he was reported to be living in Portages de Sioux north of St. Louis. He finally returned to Santa Fe in 1803, where he lived until his death in 1814.

As Vial's life was nearing its end, the power of the Spanish Empire in North America also began to wane. Spanish officials failed to uphold their end of the treaty, falling short in their supply of promised gifts and trade goods. As a result, Comanches once again mounted raids on Spanish settlements. The major target of these raids was horses to trade to Anglo-Americans, like Philip Nolan, entering Texas from the United States. This new trade market proved profitable for the Comanches, opening up to them such items as arms and ammunition and, in return, providing a steady market for their growing herds of horses.

The Spanish, fearing the erosion of control in the region, commissioned an armed foray into Comanchería to assert authority and to serve as warning to American trespassers. In 1808, sixty-nine-year old Captain Francisco Amangual— veteran of the *presidios* at Béxar and La Bahía, famous soldier and Indian fighter—led two hundred presidial and militia troops from San Antonio to Santa Fe. Traveling from early April to late December, he traversed the familiar crossings of the San Saba and Colorado before making his way atop the Caprock and across the Llano Estacado. He returned to San

Antonio the following year by way of El Paso, having made the largest circuit of West Texas in Spanish history.

The Comancheros

In place of efforts to gain a sustained peace with the Comanches, Spanish policy turned toward more a more profitable relationship—trade. The difficulty with trade had always centered on the fact that Comanchería was a vast, dangerous frontier, in which sustained Spanish presence proved problematic. Out of the 1780s peace treaties, however, the Spanish government decided to license independent merchants to conduct trade with the Comanches and Kiowas in Western Texas. They called these traders the Comancheros.

The Comancheros had a positive economic impact on the region. Their numbers increased steadily into the nineteenth century, making the Comanches and Kiowas important economic forces on the Texas plains. Initially, trade centered on Comancheros providing cloth, pots, pans, paint, beads, and hoop iron for making metal arrow heads. The Indians provided, primarily, buffalo hides. Eventually, the Comancheros added guns and liquor to their trade items, increasing the Indian dependence on these transactions.

A major drawback of the Comanchero system was an increase in Comanche kidnappings. Comanches often captured Indians from other bands or tribes, and sold them to the Comancheros for the New Mexico slave market. This activity proved so profitable that the Indians steadily increased the numbers of kidnappings. They also expanded the markets by abducting children from ranches and selling them to the Comancheros, who would ransom them back to their families for significant profits.

Clearly, Comanchería remained a dangerous borderland, not easily subdued by Spanish arms or trade. The Spanish sphere of power stopped where the frontier began; the Comanche sphere continued to increase. The borders and limits of these various spheres became increasingly cemented in the decades that followed. The Comanches raided the Spanish settlements to the south then retreated into their grassy empire, secure that they alone had the knowledge and understanding to live in such a hostile and unpredictable land. Forays to the south netted plunder and glory that would be carried back to the hostile safety of Comanchería. Eventually, the Spanish faded away, replaced by their progeny, the Mexicans, in 1821. From the Comanche perspective, this change of name altered none of the reality. The natural borders laid down by the Creator served as a convenient divider between peoples as well.

The situation would remain relatively stable until the Mexicans introduced a new contender for supremacy on the plains. This challenger would come from the East, settlers seeking what they identified as God's manifest destiny for them—the lands of Texas.

Chapter Two
Settlements, Forts, and Soldiers, 1821-1861

The Texas *frontera* caused considerable grief for the Spanish politicians in Mexico City. The obvious problem was that the Comanches dominated the region, and the government did not have the resources—human or financial—to regain control of the region. The situation had deteriorated to the point that Comanche raiders in Texas, trading their plunder to Comancheros from New Mexico, emerged as one of the principal suppliers of trade goods to the Spanish inhabitants west of the Pecos. Simply stated, Indians became major importers of items ranging from cattle to household goods, clothing, captives, and even books, all taken in raids in northern Mexico and Texas. New Mexicans depended upon this trade network, even though it was built upon the blood and misery of their fellow countrymen.

To help regain its grip, Spain turned to a system that had met with success in the past: defensive colonization. By moving populations into troubled regions, Spain had created a borderland that blunted the power of *los Indios Barbaros*, an official reference to any native beyond the scope of civilization, and dangerous foreigners. In days past, Spain had used so-called civilized Indians, or *Gente de Razón*, colonials from

The Army
Arrives

Map labels:

99° 98°

Arkansas River

North Canadian River

CANADIAN BREAKS

Cimarron River

PALO DURO CANYON

INDIAN TERRITORY

Fort Cobb, 1859

Battle of the Wichita Village, 1858

Camp Radziminski, 1858

Canadian River

Washita River

WICHITA MOUNTAINS

Fort Arbuckle, 1852

Prairie Dog Town Fork Red River

Pease River

LLANO ESTACADO

Battle of the Pease River, 1860

Wichita River

Red River

Salt Fork Brazos

Little Wichita

Camp Cooper, 1856

Comanche or Upper Reserve

Ft. Belknap, 1851

Jacksboro

Double Mountain Fork

Clear Fork

Brazos or Lower Reserve

Galconda Weatherford

Ft. Worth, 1848

Ft. Phantom Hill, 1851

BUFFALO GAP

Ft. Chadbourne, 1852

Buffalo Hump's Camp, 1853

Sanaco's Camp, 1853

Camp Colorado, 1857

Moore's Attack, 1840

Brazos River

M. Concho River Concho River

Ketumsee's Camp, 1853

TEXAS

Ft. McKavett, 1852

San Saba River

Ft. Mason, 1851

Colorado River

N. Llano River

99° 98°

elsewhere in the empire, or Catholic immigrants to perform such duty. Authorities had settled San Antonio, for example, with Canary Islanders and Tlaxcalan Indians, along with converted and educated Coahuilatecans. Catholic Germans, Irish, and Spanish colonials, with royal permission, colonized areas in Spanish Louisiana. Ultimately, military and political upheavals undermined the system, and old and reliable sources of populations disappeared or became impractical.

In 1818 a new proposal made its way to Mexico City, hand-carried by Moses Austin, an American who had first settled in Spanish Missouri. He proposed to the Spanish government that Catholic American "colonists" be allowed to settle in Texas, and become loyal, law-abiding Spanish citizens. Authorities viewed the idea with suspicion, given American proclivities toward expanding their national borders, but Catholics were clearly a persecuted sect in the United States. Religion, Spanish leaders reasoned, might be a bond stronger than nationalism. After months of studying the issue, Spain agreed to allow Austin to bring in colonists.

Other forces intervened. Moses Austin never got the chance to handle this chore for Spain for he died before he could advance the scheme. At almost the same time, Spain lost control of Mexico as that colony declared its independence in 1821. Even so, the need for a hardy and determined population on the northern *frontera* remained. When Moses' son Stephen vowed to continue his father's work, the Mexican government agreed, opening the doors to thousands of American settlers—both legal and illegal—over the next fifteen years.

Calling themselves "Texians," these fresh arrivals were a breed apart. The Comanches noticed that, unlike their rivals of previous years, these fair-skinned newcomers were less inclined to recognize borders, real and imagined. The Comanches quickly named these implacable rivals "the ones who always follow us home" and marveled at their numbers and innovation. By 1835 these industrious white men had replaced the Mexicans as the Comanche's closest neighbors, and American immigrants outnumbered the original Spanish-speaking inhabitants twenty to one.

Texas Rangers

The settlers and the Comanches witnessed the tone and tenor of their relationship on the Texas frontier change dramatically only two years after Austin began to bring his colonists to the region. In 1823 Austin hired ten experienced frontiersmen as "rangers" to ride on a punitive expedition against a band of Indians and preemptively war against hostile groups.

In 1835 Texas delegates at the revolutionary convention, gathered at San Felipe de Austin, formalized the organization known as the Texas Rangers. This force consisted of fifty-six men divided into three companies, all of whom had to provide their own mounts, equipment, arms, and rations. According to the legislation drafted by the convention, they had to be ready to ride at all times, equipped "with a good and sufficient horse . . . [and] with one hundred rounds of powder and ball."

The presence of Indians in Texas and its reaction to them would soon shape its political destiny. By 1836 the Anglo-Celtic majority in Texas fought and won a war for Independence, creating the Republic of Texas. While desire for self-government drove the revolt, other major grievances they protested included a desire to control the Indian population as they saw fit. Ironically, the belligerents exchanged their first shots of the war while fighting over a cannon once given by Mexican authorities to the settlers as protection from Indians. With independence, the frontier was now solely their responsibility.

Despite this development, the Comanches clung to their belief that distance and nature would keep these clever white men out of western Texas. In fact, such belief was well founded and widely shared. Most Texians and their American kinsmen considered the lands occupied by the Comanches and other Plains Indians as uninhabitable. Maps proclaimed this region "The Great American Desert," and what had been a boundary of climate and culture now became a geographical boundary as well. Americans were farmers, and Comanche lands would never suit agriculture. This did not keep both sides from raiding each other, though. The lands along the upper reaches of the Colorado and Brazos Rivers were borderlands now more than ever.

The president of the Republic determined the official attitude of the new nation towards its native inhabitants. Sam Houston attempted to establish peaceful relations with all Indians. This, not surprisingly, led to confusion among the

From *The Life of General Albert Sidney Johnston* (State House Press, 1997)

Indian Council at San Antonio, Texas circa 1840

tribes contacted, especially among the already suspicious Comanches who were simultaneously experiencing a steady crescendo of violence at the hands of Texas Rangers and armed volunteer militia companies. By the time these distant and highly dispersed Indians had organized to treat for peace with the Republic of Texas, a new regime had arrived to further cloud the situation.

Beginning in 1838, Texas President Mirabeau B. Lamar steadily reversed Houston's efforts and created an environment decidedly hostile to Indians. Even so, the southernmost Comanches—the Penateka—answered a call for a parlay to be held at the council house in San Antonio, still operating under the assumption that earlier peace overtures remained valid. On March 19, 1840, after rancorous debates and arguments regarding the return of white captives, fighting erupted. Texan citizens broke into the meeting and killed the attending Penateka leaders in what was seen by the Comanches not only as an outrage but diplomatic treachery.

Blood would flow on both sides that year. Indians retaliated for the council house fight by raiding all the way to the coast and sacking the towns of Victoria and Linnville in August. On their way back, this six-hundred-warrior party fought a running battle against Rangers and militia along Plum Creek. In October, Colonel John Henry Moore and around a hundred Rangers, volunteers, and Lipan allies located and destroyed a Penateka village between present-day Ballinger and Colorado City. By the end of the year, Comanches and Texans were blood enemies. Names like Jack Hays, Addison Gillespie, and Sam Walker approached heroic proportions, as did those of Buffalo Hump, Santa Anna, and Sanaco.

Raids begot raids as both sides crossed the invisible border to visit mayhem on their enemies. Because of distance, nature, and time, neither side could exterminate the other, but the weight of numbers was against the Indians. The once supreme rulers of Comanchería now began to doubt their own future prosperity and sought a negotiated settlement. The principal concession they desired was a real and permanent boundary between the warring peoples. The Texans refused.

Indian policy would take another turn in 1845. The Republic ended that year with its annexation to the United States; another view of Indians now arrived. Decades before, the American genius President Thomas Jefferson, while contemplating the purchase of the Louisiana Territory, had reasoned that the vast grassy domain of the Great Plains would serve as an "Empire for Liberty" and predicted that forty generations would pass before this corner of creation was subdued. Until that time, he believed, it would do as a homeland for the Indians—an incubator of sorts while these tribes came to know the wonders and virtues of American civilization. Thus he addressed a question that had long bothered Americans, namely, the status of Indians in the nation. This Jeffersonian view became institutionalized as a "Permanent Indian Frontier," and the United States Army become responsible for patrolling and enforcing this border. This policy would now be implemented in Texas.

Even so, Texans were not ready to concede all of their frontier protection to the U.S. government. The Rangers had built a reputation as a tough, efficient fighting unit. The U.S.–Mexican War (1846-1848), a result of the annexation of Texas, only enhanced this view of the Rangers as they were particularly adept at partisan and anti-guerilla operations. After the war, frontier defense was officially the responsibility of the United States, but the Ranger tradition would remain strong in the state.

When U.S. troops arrived to mark off the frontier line through western Texas, there were hopes and expectations from both sides that a new age had dawned. Despite all of the idealistic good intentions of the U.S. government and its frontier constabulary army, eager settlers and restless young warriors would bedevil their mission. Even though the Lone Star joined the American constellation, the Comanches continued to mark a clear difference between Texans and Americans. They would not attack Americans, but Texans were another matter entirely.

The Frontier Forts

The U.S. Army toiled on, determined to establish peace in this new region. To secure the frontier, however, the U.S. Army needed a permanent physical presence. Scouting parties and trading forays would make little impact on the balance of power in the borderlands region—the Comanches had power and presence, the U.S. did not. In the late 1840s the U.S. War Department decided to build a line of forts from the Red River to the Rio Grande to reverse this situation and to project influence onto the southern plains. In only a half dozen years there would be a second generation of forts a hundred miles farther west, more accurately reflecting the frontier line.

In June 1851 Bvt. Brig. Gen. William G. Belknap founded the northern anchor of this second line of forts. Located in Young County, the post sat near springs of the Brazos River. Capt. C.L. Stephenson commanded the four companies of the Fifth Infantry who built the original picket structures—buildings of upright poles and logs, chinked with sticks and branches woven together and usually roofed with canvas and later cedar shakes. These temporary quarters would eventually be replaced with barracks made of stone.

Watercolor of Fort Phantom Hill by J.B. Miller

Throughout the 1850s Fort Belknap served as an important military asset in protecting settlers from raiding Kiowa and Comanche Indians. The fort housed companies from the Fifth and Seventh United States Infantries, the Second United States Dragoons, and the Second and Sixth United

States Cavalries. From this northern position, the garrison could mount expeditions as far north as the Kansas plains in pursuit of raiding Indians. Fort Belknap bustled in the 1850s, offering safety and spurring significant settlement in the counties surrounding it. The fort became the hub of a network of roads going in all directions from its location, including the Butterfield Overland Mail Route in the late 1850s.

The next installation, about fifty miles southwest of Fort Belknap, was known as Fort Phantom Hill. Officially named the "Post on the Clear Fork of the Brazos," the fort came into being in November 1851 with the work of five companies of the Fifth Infantry under the command of Lt. Col. John J. Abercrombie. From the beginning, the location on the Clear Fork of the Brazos, near its junction with Elm Creek in present Jones County, was a major problem.

The fall and winter of 1851 proved to be unusually wet, giving the fort's founders the impression that the spot was markedly fertile and well-supplied with water. They began construction, but soon discovered that resources were not as plentiful as had been believed. Although they had a quarry for stone supply, they had to haul most materials to the site from miles away. The builders did their best, constructing the foundations and chimneys from stone. The rest of the buildings, however, they built of wood. The most serious difficulty proved to be the water supply. Near the fort, the Clear Fork was excessively brackish, and, to make matters worse, it turned out that Elm Creek spent much of its existence as a dry creek bed. Even when they dug a deep well, the soldiers discovered that it would not provide for the fort's inhabitants. In the end they had to haul water in barrels from a spring four miles away.

The only bright spot for soldiers was that they had relatively peaceful relations with the neighboring Indian groups. The other shortcomings of the fort, however, meant that its usefulness would come into serious question. By early 1854 the garrison at Fort Phantom Hill had been reduced to one company. Finally, in April of that year, the Department of the Army gave the order to abandon the fort. As the soldiers departed, they gleefully set the buildings on fire, hoping that no one would ever be tempted to return them to the desolate spot.

The next fort south in the line enjoyed more success. On October 28, 1852, two companies of the Eighth Infantry established Fort Chadbourne on Oak Creek in present Coke County, about sixty miles southwest of Fort Phantom Hill. They named the post for 2d Lt. Theodore Chadbourne, who had been killed at the Battle of Resaca de la Palma during the war with Mexico.

Although the soldiers at Fort Chadbourne found few of the difficulties encountered by those garrisoned at Phantom Hill, they did have to deal with one problem the men to the north did not—hostile Indians. Even though area natives came to the post to trade, the soldiers of Fort Chadbourne found themselves in several deadly contacts with these same Comanches throughout the 1850s. Some of the violence occurred quite close to the fort. In one incident, a soldier was returning to his barracks from a saloon located just off the post and across Oak Creek. As he stumbled across the bridge, Comanches filled the drunk with arrows. Miraculously, he survived. Not long afterward, Comanches captured two mail carriers on their way to the fort. The Indians burned them to death.

Chadbourne's commander, Major Seth Eastman, decided to deal more decisively with these perpetrators. He sent word to area bands inviting them to the fort for trade, games of chance, and horse races. What he actually planned, however, was to arrest suspected militants upon their arrival. When the Comanche raiders entered the post grounds, Eastman gave the signal to seize them, but he did not expect their spirited resistance. The result was a bloody firefight in which ten principal Comanche warriors died. As demonstrated by these turbulent circumstances, Fort Chadbourne remained one of the important posts in the frontier line of defense.

Military planners built Fort Mason, the next position in the line, about ninety miles southeast of Fort Chadbourne. In the summer of 1851 U.S. Army Lt. Col. William J. Hardee chose the site for the military installation in what was then Gillespie County (now Mason County). He chose a spot on Post Oak Hill, which overlooked both Comanche and Centennial Creeks. Hardee left two companies of the Second Dragoons, under the command of Bvt. Maj. Hamilton Merrill, to build the fort.

During the next decade, various units occupied the fort, protecting settlers from the Comanches, Lipan Apaches, and

Kiowas that moved through the area. The fort reached its height in 1856, when the Second Cavalry headquarters based there. The post hosted six cavalry companies under the command of Col. Albert Sydney Johnston. Like Johnston, nineteen other officers who were stationed at Fort Mason in the 1850s would rise to the rank of general during the Civil War, including Robert E. Lee, Edmund Kirby Smith, George H. Thomas, and John Bell Hood.

Also during the 1850s, the army built two other outposts near Fort Mason to allow a wider coverage in the frontier borderland area—Camp Colorado and Camp San Saba. Camp Colorado was first established temporarily near present-day Ebony in Mills County in 1855. But in August 1856, troopers of the Second U.S. Cavalry under the command of Maj. Earl Van Dorn moved the camp to a site six miles north of the Colorado River in Coleman County, and about forty miles north of Fort Mason, on a direct line between that post and Fort Belknap. The camp remained there for less than a year because of sickness among the troops. In July 1857, they relocated the camp about twenty-two miles north to Jim Ned Creek.

After settling in, Camp Colorado flourished from 1857 to 1861, becoming a center for Coleman County's settlement efforts. Soldiers built permanent structures of adobe walls and shingled roofs, hauling the lumber from the pine forests of East Texas with teams of oxen. They even strung a telegraph line along Wire Road from the camp to Army headquarters in San Antonio. Soldiers from the camp found constant work, and played a significant role in patrols and campaigns against the Comanches.

A variety of commanders followed Van Dorn in succession at Camp Colorado, all destined to gain later fame in the Civil War—Edmund Kirby Smith, John Bell Hood, and Fitzhugh Lee. Robert E. Lee also visited the camp at least twice in tours of inspection.

The second camp radiating from Fort Mason was Camp San Saba. Located only a few miles west of the old Spanish Presidio San Sabá, and about thirty-five miles west of Fort Mason, Camp San Saba was built in 1852. They soon renamed it Fort McKavett, in honor of Eighth Infantry Captain Henry McKavett who had been killed in the Battle of Monterey during the Mexican War. The post occupied more than 2,300 acres and functioned as a frontier outpost. Several companies of the Eighth Infantry occupied the fort, protecting settlers and travelers on the Upper El Paso Road. During its first few years of existence, the post grew to have the reputation of being one of the "prettiest" of the Texas forts. In 1859, however, the War Department decided to abandon the fort, leaving it to fall into disrepair.

Soldiers from the Second Cavalry established an additional military post in 1856 southwest of Fort Belknap on the Clear Fork of the Brazos River in south central Throckmorton County. Named for U.S. Army Adjutant General Samuel Cooper, the stone and picket post became the headquarters for four companies of the Second Cavalry under the control of first-time commander Lt. Col. Robert E.

Lee. Troops from Camp Cooper engaged in numerous actions against hostile Indians and served as protectors and enforcers as Comanches moved to a reservation in the area. The post closed forever in early 1861.

Robert S. Neighbors and the Indian Reservations

Once the U.S. military had established its line of forts, the next step in controlling the Comanches and other tribes on the frontier was to contain their movement. This effort would not come easily without planning and work from individuals who knew the Indians best. Robert Simpson Neighbors would fit this description, playing a major role in changing the relationship between Indians and whites on the frontier.

Neighbors was born in Charlotte County, Virginia, in 1815. After leaving Virginia at age nineteen, he arrived in Texas in the Spring of 1836. He served in the Republic of Texas Army. In 1845 he was appointed Indian Agent of Texas. One of his major innovations in this office was what he called a field system of Indian control. He was appalled to find out that the customary function of his office was to base at headquarters and wait for the Indians to come to him. Instead, he decided to deal directly with the Indians in their own territory. This practice gave him tremendous influence with a variety of plains tribes on the Texas frontier.

After Texas joined the Union, Neighbors received an appointment from the federal government as special Indian agent. He took part in several peace negotiations throughout the rest of the decade. He then fell victim to partisan politics.

In 1849, when the Whig administration of Zachary Taylor came to the U.S. presidency, they fired Neighbors, a Democrat.

After working in various jobs for the state of Texas, Neighbors turned his attentions to politics. Elected to the Texas Legislature in 1851, Neighbors became a strong voice for focus on the frontier Indian situation. Because of his influence, the legislature passed a law he sponsored making the creation of reservations a legal solution to Indian control and authorizing the use of state lands for that purpose.

When Democrat Franklin Pierce took over the presidency in 1853, Neighbors once again received appointment as the federal Supervising Agent for Texas Indians. He used the position to work toward creation of Indian reservations on the frontier. In 1854 he joined Randolph Barnes Marcy's expedition through Northwest Texas with the intention of finding suitable locations for the reservations. The result of his effort was a new state law creating two: the Comanche Indian Reservation, in what is now Throckmorton County, and the Brazos Indian Reservation in current Young County.

The Comanche reserve was to have more than 18,500 acres adjacent to Camp Cooper on the Clear Fork of the Brazos. Neighbors helped negotiate a treaty with the Penateka Comanches on August 30, 1855, sending 450 Penateka to the location to learn farming techniques. Neighbors had selected the location because it also had good hunting and water. The primary village was on the bend of the river, and it hosted several hundred Comanches and their chief, Ketumsee.

At first, the success of this social experiment looked positive. Indian Agent John R. Baylor sent a farmer and his assistant to teach the Comanches agricultural techniques, and within the first year, they had successful crops in corn, melons, peas, beans, and other vegetables. In successive years, however, drought struck, causing massive and discouraging crop failures for the novice planters.

Further trouble developed when northern bands of Comanches and errant Kickapoos raided the white settlements near the reservation; the reservation Penateka naturally received the blame. Further difficulties came from division within the Penateka themselves. War Chief Sanaco rallied many Penateka into resistance against the U.S. military, and he departed the reservation with the majority of the band following him.

Amid this deteriorating situation, Neighbors remained a tireless advocate for the remaining Penateka. He hounded the commanders at Camp Cooper over the ineffective action of the Second Cavalry in protecting settlers from insurgent Indians who were ruining the reputation of those still on the reservations. When his subordinate, Baylor, argued that perhaps not all reservation Indians were indeed trustworthy and might be guilty as suspected, Neighbors fired him and charged him with financial malfeasance. Baylor left, a bitter and vocal enemy of the reservation Indians and their protector. Try as he might, Neighbors was losing control.

Similar problems existed with the other reservation created in 1854—the Brazos Indian Reservation. Located twelve miles south of Fort Belknap, the Brazos Indian Reservation was to be home to a variety of different tribes from the northern stretches of the Texas frontier. Caddo, Andarko, Waco, and Tonkawa villages made up the nearly 37,000 acre reservation with a population of nearly 2,000 Indians. All of these tribes moved to the reservation willingly, seeing it as the main opportunity for protection against raiding Comanches.

The reservation had early success. More than six hundred acres went into cultivation, and the Indians proved to be good farmers. Area settlers generally expressed approval of the efforts of the Brazos Reservation Indians. But within a few years, minor thefts on settlers' farms and ranches led to accusations against the reservation Indians. Once again, Neighbors blamed the troops at Fort Belknap for not protecting the settlers from roaming marauders and protecting the peace of the reservation inhabitants.

By 1858 the situation grew to a fever pitch. A Jacksboro newspaper, the *White Man*, constantly published editorials blaming the reservation Indians for all depredations in the region. More importantly, the writer suggested that hostile Indians simply used the reservations as safe refuges and bases of supply close to white settlements. Fearing that the reservation experiment had been a failure, the government ordered a survey of possible sites for relocation of the two reserves north of the Red River in Indian Territory.

Before anything could be arranged, however, two incidents brought the conflict to a head. In December 1858, a resident of the Brazos Reservation, Choctaw Tom, received permission to go with a party of seventeen for a week's hunt in Palo Pinto County. Camping on Ioni Creek, they were only a few miles from the principal settlement and trading post in the county, Golconda (present-day Palo Pinto). On the night of December 26, the Indians were attacked as they slept. When dawn broke the next day, seven Indians lay dead in their blankets, and four others had serious wounds.

This was murder, and U.S. authorities moved to take action. Troops from Fort Belknap, under the command of Capt. J.B. Plummer, arrived promptly at the Brazos Reserve Agency to provide protection from further attacks while agent Neighbors arrived to conduct an investigation. He discovered that the culprits had been white men from Erath County, easily secured their names, and arranged for an examining trial in Waco. State officials never issued indictments.

Tensions escalated once again in May 1859, when Baylor arrived at the Brazos Reserve with several hundred whites in tow. He announced that he had come for certain Indians, and if the U.S. troops interfered with his action, he would treat them as hostile and fire upon them. After a tense standoff, Baylor retreated with his men, killing an elderly Caddo couple working in their garden for spite. Indian warriors bent on revenge, escorted by U.S. troops, set after Baylor and pursued him several miles to his base at the Marlin Ranch.

The Indian pursuers intercepted the Texans before they could even grab a meal or rest from their expedition. Baylor's men took defensive positions in the ranch cabins while to their front they could see both Indians and troops from Fort Belknap. The U.S. soldiers drew off, out of range, claiming no authority over the Indians while they were off the reservation. Free to exact their revenge, the Indians launched a day-long gun battle with Baylor's men while the U.S. troops watched. By the end of the day, neither side had gained an advantage, but Indian Chief Hatterbox was dead, as were two of Baylor's men.

With this increasing violence, and facing indifference from both U.S. and state officials, Neighbors decided to cut his losses and declared the Texas reservation experiment a failure. He directed the immediate removal of Indians from both the Brazos and Comanche Indian Reservations to north of the Red River. By the end of July, both groups gathered at the Red River, and on September 1, 1859, Neighbors delivered them all to officials in Indian Territory.

For Neighbors, this would be his last action on behalf of the Texas Indians. On his return, the agent stopped at the town of Fort Belknap on September 14. While visiting friends in town, Edward Cornett, a local settler, walked up to Neighbors and shot him with a shotgun at close range without warning. Neighbors died almost immediately. Supporters buried him in the civilian cemetery at Fort Belknap.

Delaware Indians

As the army arrived in Texas, it was greatly aided by the employment of friendly Indians. One of the most-used groups in this effort were the Delawares. Known as the "old grandfather tribe," this nation originated from lands along the Delaware River in the region that would become Pennsylvania, New Jersey, and New York. They were among the first Indian groups to have contacts with Europeans in America. As the white population of the eastern seaboard increased, and its westward migration ensued, the Delawares began a long process of relocation just ahead of the white advance. They moved to Ohio, then Indiana, and then Illinois. One band of the Delawares left the main group for Spanish Missouri, then Northeast Texas in the early nineteenth century, following much the same pattern as early white settlers.

The Texas experience for these Delawares would be varied, but the tribe showed a penchant for perseverance and innovation. The Spanish granted them land in Northeast Texas, title to which the Mexican government confirmed in the 1820s. Once settled, the Delawares gained a reputation as being skilled at woods and plains craft and were well respected for their significant knowledge of all aspects of the Texas plains. When Texas gained its independence, President Sam Houston granted them retention of their land titles, and the Delawares served as scouts for many Ranger expeditions against the Comanches and other tribes. When Mirabeau B. Lamar gained the presidency, he reversed Houston's friendly policies toward the Delawares and they suffered terribly in the tragic Cherokee War of 1839. As a result the Delawares and all other East Texas immigrant tribes–including Caddos, Cherokees and Shawnees—became refugees, many moving further west into Wichita and Comanche lands or north of the Red River.

Delaware fortunes improved once Houston regained the presidency. He arranged the 1843 Bird's Fort Treaty with the few remaining Texas Delawares, allowing them to settle between the Bosque and Brazos Rivers on the Northwest Texas frontier. Once again the Texas Delawares' great knowledge of the plains made them valuable assets as guides and interpreters in the region. They were even instrumental in bringing about the 1844 council between Texas government officials and the Comanches.

Once Texas entered the United States, the Delaware Indians would continue in this cooperative role. During the Mexican war, Delaware leader Jim Ned led Texas Rangers on attacks against Indians, while Black Beaver organized a volunteer company of Delaware Indians for the U.S. Army. Other Delawares would continue in similar roles throughout the 1850s—most notably, Jim Shaw, who with three other Delawares served as scout and interpreter for U.S. Army forts Belknap and Phantom Hill. The Army was grateful for this help, paying the Delawares three times more than the typical private for their services.

In the end, those Delawares who did not assimilate or work for the government ended up living among the Wichitas and Caddos on the Brazos Reservation. When the U.S. government removed Indians from the reservation in 1859, most of the remaining Delawares left for Indian Territory north of the Red River with them. Nevertheless, their assistance was one of the key components in beginning to turn the tide of control of the frontier borderland to the U.S. government.

Randolph Barnes Marcy

One military beneficiary of Delaware assistance on the Texas frontier was Randolph Barnes Marcy, one of the most respected military explorers of the West in the nineteenth century. He also illustrates the other functions the U.S. Army served while in Texas. Not only were they peacekeepers and enforcers, they were explorers, anthropologists, scientists, and naturalists intent upon exploring this region, identifying and exploiting its resources and integrating it into the nation.

Born in Massachusetts in 1812, Marcy graduated from West Point in 1828. His military career brought him to Texas in 1846 under the command of General Zachary Taylor. He served in several Mexican War battles before returning to Texas in 1847. He then set out on a military career path that would make him famous as a frontier explorer and the authority of life on the plains.

Marcy's first major mission was to chart a course from Fort Smith, Arkansas, to Santa Fe. He led an expedition to do this in 1849, successfully marking what would become known as the Marcy Trail. In 1851 the army used Marcy's skills to scout locations for the line of forts on the Texas frontier.

In 1852 Marcy embarked upon his most famous expedition. He led a large force charged with finding the source of the Red River. He and his men covered more than a thousand

Randolph Barnes Marcy as portrayed at Frontier Texas

miles of ground that had never been charted, traveling through the high plains into the Rocky Mountains. The journey was a success on many levels. They located the source of the Red River and also identified new plant and animal species and located important water sources. They even noted the location of a huge prairie dog town. Further, Marcy and his men learned important information about the previously somewhat mysterious Wichita Indians, and he even recorded information about the famous white captive, Cynthia Ann Parker, and her life with the Comanches. Upon Marcy's return, his published report made him famous as the major authority on western Texas in the 1850s.

Marcy's military career and service in Texas continued through most of the rest of the decade. He surveyed the land for the two Indian reservations and explored the headwaters of the Big Wichita and Brazos rivers. He left Texas to join in military actions in Florida and then Utah. But his 1859 publication of *The Prairie Traveler*, a fascinating guidebook for the westward traveler, cemented his reputation as *the* authority on the West. His actions in the 1840s and '50s were among the most important in establishing a strong U.S. military presence on the Texas frontier.

Buffalo Hump, Santa Anna, Ketumsee, and Sanaco

For the Comanches, the period following Mexican independence and the Texas Revolution ushered in a steady decline as they fought for dominance in the frontier borderlands of

Texas. Their nomadic lifestyles and the ferocity of their determination to conquer the region put them firmly at odds with the increasing populations coming from the East. The story of their interactions with these plains interlopers, and their strategies for survival, are best illustrated through four of their chiefs—Buffalo Hump, Santa Anna, Ketumsee, and Sanaco.

Born in either the late 1700s or early 1800s in the region near present-day Abilene, all of these men rose to power as respected men of the Penateka band of Comanches. Buffalo Hump first appeared on the historical record in 1836, but his name became firmly implanted in Texas minds in 1840 when he helped lead Comanches in the raid against Linnville and Victoria. He also played a major role in fighting Texas Rangers at Plum Creek before he escaped back to the interior of the frontier to his home on the upper Colorado River.

Despite his bellicose reputation, Buffalo Hump also demonstrated a diplomatic flair. In 1844 he entered into negotiations with the Republic of Texas government to establish a permanent treaty line between whites and Comanches. Although those negotiations failed, Buffalo Hump returned the next year to participate in the Comanche Peak Treaty and then the Council Springs Treaty of 1846. In both negotiations, Buffalo Hump served with Mopechucope, his mentor, as the principal chiefs. The success of these treaties led further to the German-Comanche Treaty signed in 1847 in Fredericksburg.

Santa Anna had also been a signer of the German-Comanche Treaty because he had been impressed with the power of the white enemy. Santa Anna had avoided much of the fighting surrounding the Linnville Raid, and he urged a more peaceful course for the Penateka. In 1846 he had traveled to Washington, D.C., to meet President James K. Polk. This visit convinced him that accommodation with the white government was essential. Polk stated that Santa Anna "thought before he came to the U.S. that his nation could whip any nation in the world, but that since he came here he found the white men more numerous than the stars, and that he could not count them."

While signing peace treaties might reduce the stature of a war chief in the minds of his people, there were other outlets to prove military prowess and to secure horses and spoils. Buffalo Hump, even while negotiating peace with Texas officials, led several raids into Mexico. He had several motivations for these actions: not only did the plunder and prestige gained from these raids solidify his following among the Penateka, but he also searched for a daughter held captive in Mexico.

By 1848, Buffalo Hump, Santa Anna, and Ketumsee lived in a village on the Clear Fork of the Brazos. The half-decade of peace-making efforts with the Texans had created a level of trust between these men and white leaders. The next year, after breaking camp for the spring, Buffalo Hump acted as a guide for John S. "RIP" Ford's San Antonio to El Paso expedition in 1849, reportedly seeing Santa Anna and several followers camped on the Pecos during that time.

While Buffalo Hump was away from his people, tragedy struck. A cholera epidemic killed many of the old chiefs in the Penateka villages, including the venerable Santa Anna. Buffalo Hump returned in 1850 to a radically different social and political environment. With little power left to resist, he reluctantly signed an agreement with the U.S. government to relocate all of the Penateka to the reservation on the Clear Fork of the Brazos. At long last there would be a clear line between whites and Indians, just not the sort hoped for by Comanches.

Ketumsee was the chief Comanche architect of this move. A contemporary to Buffalo Hump and Santa Anna, he was a steadfast and ardent advocate of peace with the whites and had signed several treaties with the Texans. A close friend of Neighbors, Ketumsee had recommended his favorite Clear Fork campsite as the natural place to locate the Comanche Reservation. He could count on the loyal support of about 180 followers and the grudging respect of several hundred more who admired his wisdom and his ability to provide security, food, and clothing owing to his cooperation with U.S. authorities. Neighbors declared him the principal chief of the Penateka. Ketumsee received a monthly salary of $30 beside his regular allotment. For this Ketumsee policed his people—identifying troublemakers and thieves—and served as guarantor of Penateka good behavior. He refused, however, to intervene in personal cases of family violence.

As tensions built between the Comanches and their neighbors, and as drought withered their crops, Ketumsee received much of the blame from all parties. The once unified Panetekas fractured into feuding factions. Many turned their devotion toward Sanaco, who had criticized Ketumsee's accommodation strategy as being tired, old, and doomed.

Penateka Comanche leader Sanaco was one of the more irreconcilable foes of Texas and Texans among his people. Born probably in the 1820s, he had become one of the primary instigators of raids along the Texas frontier. He was younger than Buffalo Hump, Santa Anna, and Ketumsee, and was known as an agitator by U.S. and Texas authorities.

His implacable nature came naturally. His father died in the Council House Fight in 1840 when Sanaco was a teenager. He was honor- and tradition-bound to avenge him, and he raided Texan farms and ranches frequently. During the violence that followed, Sanaco witnessed retaliatory raids and the systematic destruction of his people as well as the erosion of his prestige as his fellow Penatekas became war weary. Soon, all but the most hot-headed supported the advocates of peace. Now his own war with the Texans threatened to become a blood feud that would pit him against his fellow Comanches.

In the late 1840s, Sanaco had bided his time and accepted the Penateka march toward submission to U.S. authority. While not an identified signatory on the various treaties, Texan officials did identify him as living peacefully with a band of followers in a village on Spring Creek, a tributary of the Colorado, in 1849. When the southern Comanches agreed to move to the reservation on the Clear Fork of the Brazos a few years later, he went along grudgingly. There, he found himself increasingly at odds with Ketumsee. Also on the political margin among his people, Sanaco found his main strength emerging from his opposition to government authority and their chosen man. Soon an anti-reservation movement coalesced around him.

Within a year of agreeing to move to the Clear Fork, Sanaco had left. His wretched band of indigent refugees at first headed toward the Red River but soon turned west to join their cousins, the Kosoteka Comanches, as they continued a raid-and-trade relationship with whites. A few years later, he moved his band to join the Noconis where he gained a reputation as a principal actor in violence on the Texas frontier. In 1859 the Noconis were soundly defeated at the Battle of the Pease River. Sanaco, the angry Comanche, disappears from the historical record at this point.

Buffalo Hump, meanwhile, refused to choose sides in this internecine struggle, so he left Texas in 1859 with several hundred followers for the Wichita Mountains. This decision would have disastrous consequences. By leaving the reservation, Buffalo Hump was in violation of treaties he had signed with the U.S. government. Texas Rangers and U.S. troops, under the command of Major Earl Van Dorn, led an assault against Buffalo Hump's position, killing around eighty of his followers, and forcing the survivors to capitulate. Buffalo Hump—a defeated prisoner—and his remaining Penateka relocated to a new reservation north of the Red River where he was reunited with the remnant brought up from Texas. Ketumsee, their leader, would die there two years later. Buffalo Hump would never leave this reservation. He died there in 1870.

Cynthia Ann Parker

No one exemplifies the story of both sides of the Texas Frontier better than Cynthia Ann Parker. In the early 1830s, the Parkers followed the wave of settlers to Texas and had moved to the Navasota River, where they established Fort Parker as their home. In this fairly isolated area, a large force of Comanche, Kiowa, and Kichai Indians raided the fort in 1836, killing several inhabitants and capturing five. Among the captives was ten- or eleven-year-old Cynthia Ann Parker.

Although four of the captives eventually returned to their families, Cynthia would remain with the Comanches for the next twenty-five years. Cynthia grew to adulthood as a Comanche and soon became completely acculturated. Her brother, who had been captured with her, begged her to leave with him, but she refused, deciding to stay with her Comanche warrior husband, Peta Nocona. Cynthia had three children with Peta Nocona: two sons, Quanah and Pecos, and a daughter, Topsannah.

Cynthia Ann Parker may have been forgotten by the white settlers on the Texas frontier had it not been for the efforts of Indian agent Robert S. Neighbors. In 1848 Neighbors heard reports through his Comanche contacts that Cynthia was living among them. He demanded her release, but they made it clear that she could only be obtained through force. Cynthia would remain a Comanche wife and mother for another twelve years.

In 1860 Texas Rangers, under the command of Lawrence Sullivan "Sul" Ross conducted a raid on a Comanche camp

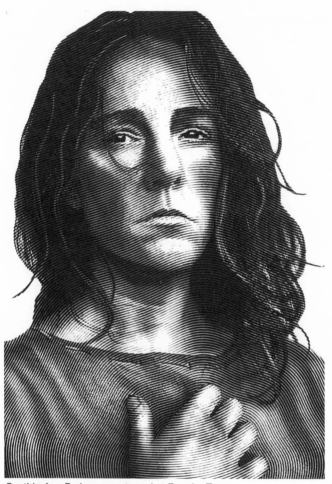

Cynthia Ann Parker as portrayed at Frontier Texas

near the Pease River. They captured three Indians but soon noticed that one of them had blue eyes. Believing that the woman might be Cynthia Ann Parker, they took her to Col. Isaac Parker, who confirmed her identity as his niece. Also with Cynthia was her daughter, Topsannah.

Cynthia was not happy about her return to white civilization. She tried unsuccessfully to escape back to her Comanche family many times but ultimately had to live out her life in a world she never really knew. She died in 1870, the same year as Buffalo Hump. Thus were gone two great icons of the early generations of Texas and Indian conflict. Even so, Cynthia Ann's son, Quanah Parker, would rise to lead the next generation of Comanches as its most prominent and influential war chief, while becoming the very embodiment of the transition of Comanches from a free people to an assimilated and controlled population.

By the end of the 1850s, the tide appeared to be turning in the balance of power on the Texas frontier. The U.S. military had effectively used Delaware scouts, intrepid explorers such as Marcy, a line of forts, and an experiment in reservations to allow settlement and to end the power of the Indians. What they could not have known was that they would have a serious setback in the coming years. Issues of frontier defense were not on the minds of politicians and soldiers back east once Abraham Lincoln was elected president. Like the feud between Sanaco and Ketumsee, but on a much larger scale, the nation of white men that had caused so much grief to the Comanches was now turning upon itself. In

December 1860 South Carolina withdrew from the Union. The resulting Civil War would mean little attention was to be paid to a frontier borderland.

Chapter Three
Ranching and the Cattle Frontier to 1861

In the mid-1850s a Methodist preacher, known to friends and neighbors as Father Tacket, moved to Boggy Creek in western Young County to set up a small ranch with his family within a few miles of the protective garrison of Fort Belknap. They owned only a few dozen head of cattle, but they made the most of the open-range conditions, allowing their herd to roam freely in the surrounding area. On January 15, 1859, Tacket was surprised to see one of his cows walking toward his cabin alone. Upon investigation, he discovered that the cow had an arrow protruding out of her neck.

He called for his three sons, Jim, George, and Lycurgus, to mount up with him to hunt for the rest of the herd. Each man armed himself with a shotgun and a revolver, then headed across the prairie. The ground lay covered in two inches of snow, allowing for easy backtracking along the path the cow had come. They found the herd two miles away at the base of a rough hill that later became known as Tacket Mountain. While keeping a wary eye on the bluff, Tacket and his sons quickly rounded up the herd and pushed them back toward ranch headquarters.

A dozen Comanches were indeed watching from the summit. As the settlers moved off, the Indians slipped quietly

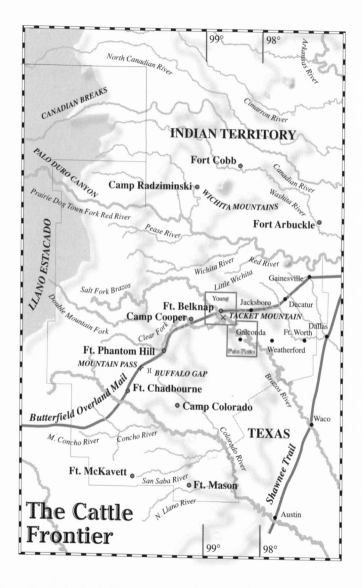

The Cattle Frontier

down the oak-studded slope and moved quickly and silently along a deep ravine to intercept the Tackets where the ditch met the path. Having arrived before their quarry, the war party dismounted, set up an ambush, and waited. After a short while, the cattle approached the crossing, but they began to stir nervously as they neared the high banks. Lycurgus Tacket assumed that a wild animal was near, so he raised his shotgun, pointing it at the gulch.

At that instant, the Comanches sprang their trap. Lycurgus pulled the trigger, spraying buckshot through the brush and dropping the only warrior armed with a gun. The other attackers closed with blades and bows, but they pulled up short and took cover as the other Tackets emptied their unaimed shotguns in the general direction of the onrushing Indians. These pellets pounded past the Indians, who wisely remained behind the protection of the gulch walls counting the blasts.

Believing that the Tackets had run out of ammunition when they fired their salvo, the Comanches threw down their bows, and renewed their violent assault with knives in hand. Only then, atop their spinning mounts and amidst their panicked cattle, did the Tackets unholster their pistols, firing with deadly effect into the oncoming assailants at close range. The Comanches had not counted on this and retreated, leaving four of their party dead. The settlers, having broken the ambush, were not unscathed. Father Tacket received a wound in the foot, while his son, Jim, had a minor wound along his eyebrow. The shaken Tacket boys quickly gathered up their cattle and headed home, casting occasional glances over their shoulders at the place where they nearly met their maker.

This brief, violent, deadly, encounter—and hundreds like it in the middle decades of the nineteenth century—illustrated one of the primary conflicts that would define the Texas frontier. Comanches had established a tenuous dominance over the region, but as the century progressed more and more settlers from the East began to crowd the buffalo ranges with cattle and horses. For a young Comanche trying to make his name, the temptation to raid these newcomers for glory and profit was irresistible.

Cattle Industry and the Open Range

Likewise, the young men who brought these animals to graze on the plains were there to make their name, as cattle have always been important to winning fame and fortune in Texas. When Spanish colonists moved into the region that is now South Texas in the 1700s, retinto (or criollo) stock often preceded them. One method of delivering the long-horned animals was to bring the cattle ships close in to land, then drive the animals off of the deck into the water where they would swim through the surf to shore. When colonists arrived in later years, these herds had increased in the wild and provided meat and leather to the needy newcomers.

American colonists drove another strain of long-horned cattle to Texas in the 1820s and 1830s. These animals, descended from English livestock, mingled with the Spanish beeves and soon produced a unique hybrid that breeders and stockmen recognized as the Texas Longhorn. Rugged, multi-colored, and armed with an impressive span of horns, these long-legged and hard-hoofed animals could travel long distances for grass and water. With their dangerous horns, they could also defend themselves from predators. Texas Longhorns multiplied rapidly after their introduction and proved to be wild, cunning creatures. They were generally more difficult to stalk and kill than buffalo or deer, and they usually roamed in groups of five or six, hiding in brushy areas by day and grazing by night. They thrived in the hostile conditions of the Texas scrub country.

Many South Texas pioneers took advantage of this hardy breed. Hipólito García established the Randado Ranch some fifty miles southeast of present-day Laredo on land granted him by the Mexican government in 1836. Vaqueros (cowboys) burned his simple "ring and ring" brand onto many a hide as his holdings and herds increased. Northeast of him, the legendary 825,000-acre King Ranch had its beginning in 1852, when Richard King and Gideon K. Lewis set up a cattle camp on Santa Gertrudis Creek near present-day Kingsville. The "Running W" brand, which first appeared in the 1860s, is still used today. Most of the ranch hands were Mexican; in fact, in 1854 King moved all the inhabitants of a drought-stricken Mexican village to his ranch and hired them. These workers came to be known as *kineños* or "King's men," and cattle made them rich.

In North Texas, Christopher Columbus Slaughter typified the style of men who were entering the region from the southern U.S. At age nineteen in 1856, he moved with his family from East Texas to the good cattle range in Palo Pinto County southeast of Fort Belknap. Here Slaughter became famous as a trail driver and Indian fighter, and his "Long-S" brand became a common sight on the Northwest Texas frontier where he would eventually earn the nickname "Cattle King of Texas."

The animal that allowed these ranchers to amass their fortunes was perfect for the conditions. Texas remained a remote frontier for most of its early existence, and persons interested in selling their animals at a profit often had to trail, or drive, these beeves hundreds of miles to market. This practice had not started in Texas. Settlers in the early American colonies had been trailing livestock to market for generations, as had their descendants in the American South. In those early days, most of the cattle drives were conducted on foot by African-American slaves expert at working cattle, including many young slaves who became known as "cowboys." By their sides were their trusty dogs, controlling the beeves by barks and bites.

The cattle industry that would find its way onto the Texas frontier was, in large part, an extension of the practices from the American South. Contrary to the precepts of popular imagination, Southern agriculture was not based simply on plantation crops. In fact, for all of the period before the Civil War, livestock was more valuable to the South than all other agricultural commodities combined. For the most part, the South was a vast wilderness with relatively few cleared and planted acres and with relatively few inhabitants. Cattle and other livestock roamed the woods unattended. For the sake of comparison, in 1850 there were twice as many acres cleared and under cultivation in the North than in the South.

These conditions, therefore, made the South perfect for the open-range system of herding which simply meant that livestock were allowed to roam freely without being limited to fenced areas of a person's property. Laws in the South favored this system, requiring farmers and planters to fence their crops if they did not wish them to be consumed by unrestrained livestock. Cattle owners did not even have to own land—their herds were allowed to graze where they wanted. Identified by a brand or earmark, cattle only had to be rounded up once or twice a year to be driven to market.

Cattle Drives and the Shawnee Trail

After Texas independence in 1836, thousands of immigrants from the American South entered the region, bringing their livestock and open-range practices with them. Texans became especially good at driving cattle. The first such drives hit the trail in the 1830s when American settlers in Austin's Colony pushed their surplus stock across the coastal prairies of Texas to Louisiana where they loaded onto steamboats for the trip to the highly lucrative New Orleans beef market. Later, Texans tried driving their cattle to northern markets in Illinois, Indiana, Ohio, Iowa, and Missouri. The first such cattle drive occurred in 1846 with a 1,000-head herd heading to Ohio.

Courtesy of Buffalo Gap Historic Village, Buffalo Gap, Texas

Woodcut of Longhorns crossing a creek

The success of such northern drives inspired entrepreneurs, such as Tom Candy Ponting, to take advantage of the opportunities presented by Texas cattle. In 1853 he and a partner came to Texas from Illinois to purchase cattle. They bought a wagon, a canvas cover that could double as a tent, and a yoke of oxen. Then they purchased six hundred steers and set out to drive them north across the Red River. To keep the steers in some sort of order, they tied a belled ox to the back of the wagon; the cattle followed. While in Indian Territory, the partners purchased eighty more steers to join their herd. After four months on the trail they reached Illinois.

The partners wintered the cattle in Illinois, but they were not yet finished with the herd. They sold most of the steers in

Chicago for a profit, but they decided to ship 150 of them by rail to New York City, where beef prices were at a premium. They considered the transaction successful, but they also learned an important lesson about transportation. It had cost them about two dollars a head to drive the cattle 1,500 miles on the hoof, but the 600-mile train ride to New York cost them seventeen dollars a head. The trail drive was still the most profitable means for the Texas cattleman.

Other entrepreneurs found success in driving their cattle west in the 1850s. In 1856 New Yorker Frederick Law Olmsted reported that he saw four hundred head of cattle being driven from San Antonio to the gold fields of California. Twenty-five men riding mules accompanied the herd. Most of these riders, however, were working only for meals, in an effort to have transportation to the gold mines of California. This venture proved extremely profitable for the cattle owners. Steers that cost fourteen dollars in Texas returned more than a hundred dollars apiece in California after only a five- or six-month trail ride.

Even though California was an occasional destination for Texas cattle, the majority of pre-Civil War Texas cattle drives traveled to the northeast on what was known as the Shawnee Trail. Long used by various Indian tribes in hunting and raiding, this trail passed through Austin, Waco, and Dallas, crossed the Red River at Rock Bluff, and proceeded northward along the eastern edge of Indian Territory. At Fort Gibson, the trail split into routes to Missouri settlements such as St. Louis, Independence, Sedalia, and Kansas City, or to Kansas destinations such as Baxter Springs. Settlers to Texas from the Midwest also followed this route southward, traditionally calling it the Texas Road. Beginning in the 1840s drovers on the Shawnee Trail referred to it as the cattle trail, the Sedalia Trail, the Kansas Trail, or simply as "the trail." References to the Shawnee Trail probably came from the passage of the route near a Shawnee village on the Texas side of the Red River.

Use of the trail increased into the 1850s, as herders took their cattle to the northern markets. In these early drives, cattle followed oxen-pulled wagons, laden with bedding and food for the cowboys. If an ox went lame, the men simply roped a steer into service to pull the wagon. Food was usually in short supply, and the men had little more than beef to eat during their journeys. Trail herds in the 1850s usually numbered only a few hundred head, with four riders for each hundred cattle. Each man usually had two or three horses, and they were at the mercy of the elements during the entire trip. If a man became separated from the wagon by nightfall, he would have to sleep on what was called a "Tucson bed"—his stomach for a mattress and his back for a blanket.

These trail drives, never numerous, almost faded away forever. In the 1850s, outbreaks of *babesiosis* or "Texas Fever"—a cattle blood disease transmitted by ticks—caused most states to close their borders to herds coming up the trail. Missouri farmers correctly identified the Texas Longhorn as the culprit in introducing this disease, but they incorrectly assumed that the cattle's breath, rather than the ticks they carried, was the problem. The hardy Texas Longhorn proved resistant to the disease resident in their parasite ticks.

Missouri farmers opposed the passage of these herds near their homes and crops, and violent encounters between sod-busters and cattlemen became more frequent. In 1855 vigilance committees formed by angry farmers emerged in central and southern Missouri. Cattlemen from the state successfully petitioned the Missouri legislature to ban diseased Texas cattle from entering the state. The law, however, proved ineffective, since the Texas Longhorns were not diseased—merely carriers of the ticks that spread the fever. By 1856 outbreaks of "Texas Fever" erupted in Kansas, leading to an official ban on Texas cattle there as well.

Despite these obstacles, several Texas cattlemen persisted in getting their herds through the region. In 1857 Jesse Day and Willis McCutcheon drove herds to Quincy, Illinois, turning handsome profits; in 1858, Palo Pinto County rancher Oliver Loving successfully trailed a herd to Illinois. The following year he reached southern Kansas with another herd, wintering them there, and then taking them along the Arkansas River to Pueblo, Colorado.

Ranches on the Range

The West Texas frontier proved to be the perfect region for those moving from the East to establish their stake in the cattle business. Steeped in the traditions of the Southern herding system, the frontier offered the largest open range any of them had ever seen. By the 1850s, when the U.S. military moved into the frontier region to establish its line of forts, the situation looked even better for ranchers. The military offered protection for them and their families, and the military provided an economic incentive. The thousands of soldiers living in the forts needed to be fed, so government beef contracts became a major economic boom, especially for frontier cattle raisers. Nevertheless, they faced tremendous difficulties getting their ranches started in this borderland area, including problems with housing, cattle ownership identification, and, as the Tackets learned, Indians.

Upon arriving on the Great Plains of West Texas, settlers found their most immediate and daunting challenge to be housing. Rugged cattlemen and their families were faced with the stark reality that this new land looked nothing like the great wooded terrain they had left. Occasional mesquite thickets or cedar breaks simply did not offer the material necessary to build the cabins and houses to which they had become accustomed back East.

The most basic early solution to this problem was to build temporary shelters in the very earth on which they stood. Called dugouts, these shelters could be found all over West Texas throughout the early period of frontier development. The most typical dugout consisted of a rectangular pit, five to seven feet deep, eight to ten feet wide, and of variable length. They constructed the roof from logs and branches laid across the pit. On these they placed saplings, grass, tow sacks, and any other material that could lend strength, and then they covered the whole structure with dirt. Stairs dug into the ground provided access. One variation of this type of construction was the partial dugout, which settlers carved into the sides of hills. It was favored in broken terrain.

Dugouts provided settlers with vital shelter, but they were not considered pleasant places to live. The floors were tamped earth, and everything was "dirty." Residents often complained that dirt fell constantly from the walls and ceilings onto their furnishings and into their meals. They also reported the frequent presence of snakes, spiders, and other pests in the ceiling. Perhaps the most difficulty came, however, when the occasional cow stepped onto the camouflaged roof.

After settlers were ready for more permanent housing, the next step was to build *jacales*, picket cabins, log cabins, or stone houses. The simplest of the four—the *jacal*—consisted of anchoring corner posts into the ground, then weaving together straw and branches for the walls. Similarly, picket cabins consisted first of digging a ten-foot trench about two feet deep. Into this trench builders placed the ends of several timbers until they had a wall of upright pickets. Repeating this to make four walls, the builders then packed mud and clay in the spaces between the pickets. The advantage of the picket house was that the logs used did not have to be completely uniform. The mud and clay helped to add structural integrity. For both the *jacal* and the picket cabin, settlers usually opted for a dirt roof until they had time to turn out a load of cedar shakes. Another option was to move toward the more traditional single-pen log cabin. These structures needed more uniform hewn logs that could be stacked on each other and interlaced at the corners. These cabins were possible only where settlers found a nice stand of cedars or other hardwood trees. Finally, settlers also could opt to use a building material that was in abundance in West Texas—rocks. Rock buildings provided sturdy structures, but took tremendous amounts of labor to build.

With their home place built, Texas ranchers next had to deal with the vast difficulties of differentiating their own cattle from those owned by others on the open range. The solution to this problem was a practice long employed in the southern United States and in the former Spanish regions of America—branding. Evidence that branding first came to the Americas with the Spanish is clear. Shortly after Hernán Cortés's conquest of the Aztecs in 1521, he marked a herd of cattle as his own by branding three Latin crosses into their hides. This action was most likely the first incidence of branding in the Western Hemisphere. By 1537 the Spanish crown created a cattle owners association for New Spain called *Mesta*, requiring that all stockmen brand their cattle with a unique, identifying mark and register the brand in a book in Mexico City. This practice continued into Texas as Spanish cattle owners expanded into the region in the 1700s.

Spanish branding tended to be along the lines of pictographs, rather than letters. Spanish tradition had each cattle owner design his own stylized brand, complete with the flourish of pendants and curlicues. Each generation descended from the original owner would add another pendant or curlicue to the brand, making it distinctively their own, but also making the brand more ornate.

Cattlemen from the American South had long practiced branding as well, and they brought the practice with them into their Texas ranches. Southern brands, however, tended to include initials of the owners rather than pictographs, making for some interesting blending when they came into contact with cattle branded in the traditional Spanish fashion. By the 1840s, Texans had come to refer to Spanish or Mexican brands as "dog irons," or "¿quién sabes?" (Spanish for "who knows?"). During the Republic of Texas period, the government provided for the recording of brands, but did not enforce the measure. Over the next several years, many counties began to record brands for their cattle-owning residents much like counties in the South, and in 1848 the state legislature required that county clerks begin recording brands and ruled that unrecorded brands did not constitute legal evidence of ownership.

Tradition, not law, dictated that cattle owners brand their stock on the left hip. There have been many explanations for this practice. Some claimed that cattle tended to mill more to the right than to the left, so a brand on the left hip would be more visible to cowboys at a roundup as the herds turned clockwise away from the riders. Others claimed that most ropers tended to be right-handed and would therefore generally approach the steer from the left side. A final explanation from some old cowboys was that since English is read from left to right, the brand needed to go on the left-hand side because it makes sense to read from "head to tail."

This was especially true when marks stretched the entire length of the animal. In addition to branding, stock raisers also used other types of markings to identify their cattle. Some used what was known as the wattle or dewlap, a mark made on the animal's jaw or neck by pinching up the skin and cutting it partially off. The remaining flap of skin, when healed, hung from the animal in a distinctive manner unique to the owner. More common than wattles were earmarks. A long-time tradition in the American South, this practice involved cutting a distinct notch or design in one or both ears of the steer. Most Texas cattlemen used earmarks along with their brands. In addition there were neck brands and even shoulder brands, turning some poor beeves into a veritable catalogue of ownership past and present.

With the intricacies of cattle identification handled by branding and marking, Texas ranchers faced one other, more deadly problem on the frontier—Indians. The necessity for open space for cattle operations meant that ranchers and their families tended to be isolated from others on the plains. This made them perfect targets for many of the nomadic tribes and bands that called the frontier region home. Even so, these stockmen were bred from generations of Indian fighters and many knew the intricacies of personal combat well.

Most Plains Indians were not interested in the ranchers' herds. The nomadic tribes raided onto settlers' homesteads quickly and could not be slowed down by plodding cattle. Instead, Comanches and Kiowas were much more interested in the other major asset owned by cattlemen—their horses. Indians would most often take horses in the middle of the night, avoiding, if possible, potentially deadly encounters with ranchers. While thrilling and enriching the raiders, there was only limited glory in stealing horses. On other occasions Indians sought captives or scalps along with their plunder, leading to many a life and death struggle on the frontier.

Living in this new land meant coping with the threat of a lurking enemy. Settlers watched the seasons and the cycles of the moon to try and predict when the raiders would come, but often death came unexpectedly with the swift flight of a feathered arrow. Where cattlemen were most vulnerable to Indian attacks was in the open, tending to their herds. Homesteads offered some protection from attacks, and some even had the added safety of stockade fences with firing loops. On the open plains, however, Indians often had the advantage of surprise and could pick the terrain for an ambush or attack.

An exotic and sometimes complicating factor on the frontier was the presence of millions of buffalo. The Indians relied on them as a moving commissary but resented the fact that buffalo tended to change their migration patterns in response to the presence of homesteads. Indians might have hunted the beast on a particular range for a generation only to find them gone, shying away from a steadily increasing population of settlers with their dogs, horses, cattle, and guns. Ranchers were happy to see them go, too, and often found the roaming herds of bison to be anything from a minor annoyance, as they trampled through their improvements, to a devastating presence. Millions of buffalo competed for grazing lands with the free-ranging cattle, serving as a serious deterrent to the major growth and expansion of the industry before the Civil War.

Sheep on the Frontier

Cattle culture, above all else, was king, but sheep production also made its mark on western Texas. Sheep ranching came to Texas with the first Spanish explorers and missionaries. Throughout the Spanish period, there was a steady increase in sheep herds in the province. When American pioneers started to populate Texas, they did not readily adopt sheep raising except as an adjunct to other agricultural pursuits. But by the 1850s new sheep breeds spurred interest in the industry. This renewed emphasis, however, focused on the wool rather than the mutton that sheep provide.

Sheep ranching in West Texas provided busy seasonal activities for many in the region. The most important activity was "lambing." Sheep ranchers bred their range ewes in the fall so that they would lamb between February and May. The herder had to act as midwife during lambing season, assisting in difficult births, caring for lambs born to "dry" ewes, and generally aiding the lambs through the dangerous first few weeks of life. One herder called the lambing season a "month long hell of worry and toil."

Shearing season was the next important activity in the life of a sheep rancher. On large ranches, itinerant shearing crews handled most of the work. Unlike lambing season, the shearing represented a social period for the herder—a time marked by the companionship of others. Owners used the excuse of a shearing crew's arrival to begin feasting, drinking, and visiting. But after the fun came some real work. Shearing crews worked from sunup to sundown, bent over the sheep, shearing the wool by hand. Men tied the fleece with twine, and stuffed it into a bag that was eight to ten feet long, with each bag weighing about 360 pounds. When they had sheared all sheep, the crew would then move on to the next ranch.

Ultimately, sheep did not catch on during the frontier period. Predators and climate worked against the industry, as did a lack of access to markets. Raw wool was useful in small quantities for local consumption, but it had to be hauled to mills hundreds of miles away for commercial success; neither could sheep be driven to market. Even though raising woolies never approached the breadth and depth of the cattle industry in West Texas, this often-forgotten animal did leave a light mark on the frontier and helped to shape the social and economic fabric of the region.

Butterfield Overland Mail

By the late 1850s, the United States appeared in full flower. Its domain stretched the breadth of the continent and its possessions on the Pacific Coast were booming. At the same time, the dominance of settlers over the Indians of Texas appeared assured. The second line of forts operated with some success, ranchers were overcoming the wide variety of challenges that faced them, and pioneers began transforming the prairie wilderness into the kinds of homes they hoped for their children. Nothing represented this progress more to the citizens of frontier Texas than the announcement of a continuous overland mail system through the region.

In 1857 a congressional act authorized the establishment of a mail contract to convey letters twice weekly, in both directions, between St. Louis, Missouri, and Memphis, Tennessee, in the east and San Francisco, California, in the west. The act also stipulated that four-horse coaches suitable for carrying passengers would carry the mail. A final requirement was that the trip should take no more than twenty-five days. John Butterfield and Associates won the contract, agreeing to compensation of $600,000 per year, plus receipts for passengers and express.

Butterfield began his Southern Overland Mail operation on September 15, 1858. By necessity this all-weather route wound its way through West Texas. Moving from the two eastern termini (St. Louis and Memphis), the routes converged into one at Fort Smith, Arkansas. The distance between Fort Smith and San Francisco on this route totaled 2,795 miles—probably the longest route for horse-drawn conveyances in the history of the United States. The route crossed into Texas from the Indian Territory at Sherman.

From there it moved west to Gainesville, Jacksboro, Fort Belknap, and Clear Fork Station. Other prominent West Texas stops included Fort Phantom Hill, Mountain Pass, Fort Chadbourne, Carlsbad, Pope's Camp, Hueco Tanks, and Franklin (present-day El Paso).

The Butterfield route proved quite beneficial to settlement in West Texas. Community leaders all along the route clamored to have the line stop in their town. They believed that with communication and transportation would come progress, law, and safety on the frontier. By early 1859 these communities got their wish. Butterfield made Sherman a mail distribution center, and fledgling Texas settlements west of there gained reliable postal service.

For the eastern portions of the route, the Butterfield line used Concord coaches drawn by horses. These vehicles had room for five or six passengers, although more could be found crowded in. Once across the Red River, the service changed to Celerity Wagons, a boxy but sturdy vehicle designed much like an army ambulance, and horses gave way to mules. Passengers desiring a one-way trip from Memphis or St. Louis to San Francisco could expect to pay an average of $200. The trip was quite uncomfortable, and as the coaches went through large stretches of Indian country, the journey was also dangerous. The owners encouraged passengers to travel armed in case of a hostile attack. If a passenger decided to lay over at a stop, he would lose his seat and might have to wait as long as a month before another one came available. Nevertheless, in the two and a half years of its operation, the Butterfield Overland Mail line never suffered an Indian attack in Texas, nor did it ever miss its twenty-five day travel deadline.

Secession and the Frontier

Despite all of these promising signs, the national euphoria was tempered. Sectionalism, a constitutional crisis, and issues regarding slavery bubbled and brewed to concoct a deadly toxin to this gathering prosperity. To a West Texan on a cow hunt in the Clear Fork country, with a hand on his six-shooter and another on his reins, these national trends seemed a distant distraction compared to the work at hand. Even so, the national crises would break upon him and his family as surely as they would on his cousins back in distant Tennessee and Virginia.

One of the first harbingers of this gathering doom struck what had been the most recent bearer of good news to frontier Texas. The Butterfield Overland Mail service abandoned its southern route in March 1861 when the company amended its national contract to modify the course northward. The early promise of reliable transportation and communication in West Texas collapsed. The national disruption would delay its return for decades.

Other troubling signs broke upon the frontier like waves of calamity driven by a distant hurricane. Promising cattle markets in the North closed, and even though significant numbers of Texas cattle found new markets to the east in Louisiana and later across the Mississippi River to

Confederate armies, the demand was sporadic and payment spotty. The majority of untended Longhorns roamed the brush country, profits unrealized, and simply multiplied while the trail hands left, drawn away back East—to the land they had left—and distant battlefields. Perhaps the most distressing trend, though, was the exodus of U.S. troops from the frontier forts. This day, long-anticipated by Comanches and Kiowas and long-dreaded by the settlers, presaged a violent crescendo of death on the Texas frontier.

When Texas formally seceded from the Union on February 2, 1861, the troops garrisoned in the once welcome forts were now, technically, representing a foreign government. This turn of events played out most dramatically at Fort Chadbourne. After Texas seceded, Texan Col. Henry McCulloch marched his state troops to the fort and demanded its immediate surrender. The difficulty with this situation was that the United States government of lame duck president James Buchanan did not recognize the constitutional validity of secession. All of the forts on the Texas frontier were U.S. government property, and if secession was not legal, then that status had not changed. Back in Washington, there was still hope that a peaceful solution to the secession crisis might be reached, as no bloodshed had yet occurred. McCulloch's demand for U.S. Army troops to hand over government property to an insurgent force could very well force the entire nation into a bloody standoff.

On February 28, 1861, Fort Chadbourne's commander decided that defending the post against McCulloch's men would be fruitless. He handed over the fort and marched his men out, avoiding the start of hostilities. War between North and South would have to wait another few weeks, when a similar standoff occurred in Charleston, South Carolina, at Fort Sumter.

For most of the rest of the frontier forts, U.S. troops abandoned them in an orderly fashion, leaving control to the Texas troops. At Fort Belknap, when the post commander had heard of the Texas secession vote, he ordered his troops to march for Fort Leavenworth, Kansas, leaving the post empty. Similarly, troops abandoned nearby Camp Cooper by the end of February. Most of these posts would remain vacant for the next six years, if not forever. The settlers were on their own.

Chapter Four
Civil War and the Texas Frontier, 1861-1865

The summer of 1861 was pregnant with implications for the United States. In Virginia, the two largest American armies ever assembled maneuvered, each intent upon routing the other and marching triumphantly into the enemy capital. In Arkansas and Tennessee, southern armies, including scores of Texas Rangers, plotted and planned for coming combat. Even in El Paso a man once familiar with the Texas frontier, John R. Baylor, led troops into Federal New Mexico to advance the southern cause there. In Weatherford, range-hardened veterans gathered in the town square to organize themselves for war. On the banks of the Clear Fork, George Reynolds, the son of an increasingly prosperous pioneer family, bid his cattle-raising father and brothers farewell as he too went to war, soon to serve with the Nineteenth Texas Cavalry.

As these titanic forces gathered for a cataclysmic encounter, a smaller struggle for life and death, dominance, and submission was occurring on the plains of the Texas frontier. This Texas fight, however, had been going on for centuries. It was not about issues of slavery or states' rights but about the control of a borderland region between determined cultures.

Civil War
on the
Frontier

That same July, a Young County resident named John F. Bottorff made his way from his small cabin on a clearing near Elm Creek to take a hide press, a prized yet cumbersome machine that helped flatten cow hides, to the more settled pastures of Johnson County. Bottorff had located his residence on this remote frontier because its proximity to Fort Belknap afforded relative safety from Indians. But now, Bottorff was more isolated than he had ever been living in Young County, and he was anxious to get this expensive piece of equipment out of harm's way.

He set off that morning with his wagon, bearing the press, being pulled by a yoke of four oxen. He made steady progress, traveling about thirty-five miles in the sweltering sun by mid afternoon. Sitting on the wagon tongue, Bottorff rode across a flat stretch of prairie in Jack County unaware of any danger and eager to get to safer country. As he blissfully whittled away the distance, he did so not knowing that six Indians, probably Comanche or Kiowa, had been shadowing him for the last few miles.

When he got within range of their bows, they unleashed a barrage of arrows. By chance, a few hundred yards away, another settler named Glasinjim was hunting wild horses and he witnessed the assault. Glasinjim, who was riding a mule, moved to assist the wagon driver and lend his aid in fending off the attack. Thinking that there surely would be a rifle on the wagon, he spurred his mount forward in a race to try to reach it and make a stand. Bottorff, though, was already dead. Riding swift horses, the Indians reached the wagon much faster than Glasinjim. Realizing his mistake, he turned his mule around and raced toward his home on Rock Creek a mile and a half away. The Indians gave chase and quickly closed the gap between themselves and Glasinjim's lumbering mule.

About a half mile from his house, Glasinjim knew that he would never reach its safety. He stopped his mule, pulled out his revolver, and turned quickly to face his attackers, spewing curses at them with every breath. Surprised by this turn of events, and impressed by the man's courage, the Indians halted, talked it over among themselves and apparently decided that a potential bullet wound was not worth this man's mule, pistol, or scalp. Instead, they turned back to plunder Bottorff's wagon, leaving Glasinjim alive and unharmed. Borttoff's death was just one of many in the wake of the military abandonment of the Texas frontier.

Fate of the Frontier Forts

With the U.S. Army gone, Texas scrambled to restore some semblance of protection on its exposed western border. Two of the old federal posts in the region—Fort Mason and Camp Colorado—would see some limited service during the war. Fort Mason came under the control of state troops in February 1861 but soon had to be abandoned for lack of resources from the state. Then, for a brief time in 1862, the Confederate Army returned to the rapidly decaying post, using it to house 215 prisoners, most of whom were local Union sympathizers. By the late summer, however, they abandoned the fort once again, leaving citizens in the area vulnerable to Indian attacks and lawlessness. At Camp Colorado, on the other hand, all of the U.S. troops present in February 1861 went into the Confederate service, and the camp had continuous military occupation throughout the war.

The responsibility for frontier defense fell to the Texas government, which had neither the resources nor manpower to assume it. In 1862 the state formed the Frontier Regiment, under the command of Colonel James M. Norris, as an attempt to protect frontier settlements. Norris established a chain of sixteen posts—some new, some using the buildings of old U.S. forts—stretching from the Red River to the Rio Grande. He had his men march in regular patrols along that line, with each company separated by about a day's march. This strategy had very little success, as the troops were stretched too thin to respond to any raid or real threat, and their regular patrols were easily discerned by observant Indians.

Despite its ineffectiveness the Frontier Regiment remained diligent in its attempts to perform its duty. Occasionally a detachment would come across Indians. When it did, the goal was simple—extermination. Ranger Captain R.B. "Buck" Barry commanded the patrol company based out of Fort Mason on the San Saba River. In April 1862 his men camped alongside a second company led by Captain Milton Boggess. A party of Comanche warriors made their way up the San Saba, returning from a raiding expedition into the white settlements. They were heavily laden with booty and were trailing a large number of horses.

The two companies set after them right away, chasing the Indians for ten or twelve miles before cornering them. The Comanches turned back, abandoned all of their stolen horses, and put up a ferocious fight against the Rangers. Surprisingly one of the most determined Indians was wearing a silk dress. The Rangers had never seen a woman so adept at using the bow and arrow but soon realized that the warrior was a man, who had probably taken the dress in their recent raid.

The Indians moved into a thin oak thicket and, from defensive positions, started to wreak havoc on the attacking Rangers. Their arrows killed and wounded many of Barry's men and their horses. One of his officers reeled back in pain, his lips pinned together with an arrow. Comanches, too, died in the exchange, and both sides withdrew without gaining the advantage over the other. These marauders would live to plunder again. This kind of action was rare for the Frontier Regiment; most Indian raiding parties wisely avoided traveling where patrol companies camped.

Since the state could not protect them, settlers did what they had done for years, continuing their own private war against the Indians. In March 1863 the people living in Hanna's Valley in Brown County heard reports that a small band of Indians was in the area. Ten men, led by Owen Lindsey and Albert Jones, set out to hunt them down. Armed with rifles and pistols, the men found the Indians' tracks quickly and set off in pursuit. Near the mouth of Pecan Bayou, they found eleven dismounted Indians trying to climb a steep, craggy incline. The enthusiastic but inexperienced Lindsey and Jones raced their horses ahead of the pack in quick pursuit, arriving first at the base of the hill. They charged up the near-vertical path on foot, but the Indians turned to fight from well-defended positions.

Lindsey dashed forward, but was killed almost immediately as a rock from above crashed into his skull at the same time as an arrow pierced his chest. Jones was also stopped in his path, as an arrow plunged deep into his thigh. The rest of the men arrived at the scene and started to fire at the Indians, but the defensive position of the Indians was too great, and they were able to make their escape. Blood spilled on the rocks above indicated that at least one of them had been seriously wounded in the fight. This fight, like so many, was frontier violence which accomplished little save killing a rash pioneer and condemning two other men—one white, one native—to suffer the agonies of a wound far from medical attention.

This weathered drama played out in dozens of different ways, and those seeking a new living on the frontier often learned that life was cheap in this promised land. Jeremiah Green had moved to Texas from North Carolina in 1859, settling in Hood County. He, like his neighbors, had come to the region to begin a cattle operation. In July 1863 Green and four of his neighbors went out onto the range to gather cattle. By afternoon on that sweltering day, the men and horses were parched and headed toward a stream for water and rest.

After they quenched their horses' thirst, they walked them to the top of a nearby rise to graze and rest.

Once on top of the rise, the men saw a party of sixteen Indians a few hundred yards away. The Indians also saw them, and they gathered their mounts together in a council, deciding whether they could take this handful of cow men. Green and his companions had a debate of their own— whether to fight or flee, as they only had two guns between them. Before the group made a decision, however, one of the men made up his own mind, mounted his horse, and fled. With their number down to four, two others followed this example. Green and one other man remained, both riding mules and well aware that not only were they poorly mounted, but hopelessly outnumbered.

With the odds more to their liking, the Indians took the opportunity for a little personal glory and made their attack while their intended victims spurred their inferior mounts in an attempt to escape. Knowing that the Indians were gaining, Green's companion jumped from his mule and made his escape on foot into a thick cedar brake where the Indians would at least have to hunt for him. Green, who was fifty-three years old and fairly overweight, could not duplicate the maneuver. The Indians caught him, killed and scalped him, and left his corpse on the edge of the cedar brake, all for the satisfaction of this easy victory and two mules.

Two major changes to frontier defense occurred in 1863. Texas officials fumed about having to pay for the upkeep of the Frontier Regiment and had, on several occasions, attempted to make it part of the regular Confederate army so that Richmond, not Austin, could foot the bill. The Confederate government refused unless the unit could be called to different fields to answer emergencies of national importance. Amid this impasse, in order to make such a move plausible should a compromise between state and national authority be found, Governor Francis R. Lubbock reorganized the Frontier Regiment along more formal military lines. The men elected Major J.E. McCord as the new leader of the restructured command.

McCord brought energy to his new role. He realized that the regular patrols had little effect on the increasing number of Indian raids, so he scrapped the system. He replaced it with aggressive scouting expeditions that would preemptively seek out and destroy Indian raiding parties and their camps. He hoped that with these unpredictable tactics he would have the element of surprise at the point of contact.

Typical of the effects brought by McCord's scouting strategy was an encounter in the fall of 1863. A scouting party of seven men headed toward Fort Belknap when they came across four Indians. Of the soldiers, only Jim Dozier had a rifle, the rest had pistols. Upon seeing the four Indians, Dozier immediately raised his rifle and killed one of them. The other three warriors made a hasty flight, with the pistol-toting soldiers in close pursuit. Pistols fired from running horses proved ineffective, but once Dozier had reloaded, he dropped another Indian with a bullet from his rifle. The soldiers continued to ride down the two remaining Indians, finally shooting one in the back with a six-shooter. The fourth warrior escaped.

Meeting the occasional small party of Indians with equally small scouting parties raised the stakes for the raiders. They now had to be more cautious and were wary of making their forays with too little strength. For Texans, this new approach appeared to keep the Indians off balance but promised to escalate the size and potency of their raids. At the very moment when the Comanches and Kiowas were reacting to this new reality, the Confederate States of America intervened and removed most of the veteran troops from the fight.

In December 1863 Texas politicians gave in. The Frontier Regiment became a component of the Confederate Army. This bureaucratic shift, as predicted, allowed local Confederate planners to draw away more than half of the regiment from the frontier. Officers in East Texas took advantage of the changed status and used the force to reinforce the defenses on the Texas coast to replace troops being sent further east. While this change did little to make major towns like Houston safer, it made the frontier even more perilous. Another new command, the Border Regiment, would patrol some stretches of the North Texas frontier, but its area of responsibility went almost the entire length of the Red River. Under the command of Col. James Bourland, a sixty-two-year-old veteran of the East Texas Indian wars of the Republic and notorious for his persecution of Union sympathizers in Gainesville, this unit concerned itself more with rounding up Confederate deserter conscripts than fighting Comanches.

Politicians in Austin anticipated these new conditions. Instead of leaving settlers at the mercy of the Indians, the state required that all men living in the frontier counties to enlist in a militia known as the Frontier Organization and stipulated that one-fourth of these men were to be patrolling in the field at all times. Most patrols numbered around a dozen men and could be expected to be in the field for ten days at a time. By early 1864 nearly 4,300 men had enrolled in three frontier military districts, the first headquartered at Decatur, the second at Gatesville, and the third at Fredericksburg. With the newly raised militia, the occasional sweeps by Bourland's men, and the work of remnants of the Frontier Regiment, the government reasoned, the Indian threat could certainly be contained. All of these organizations received instructions to enforce Confederate and Texas laws in their jurisdictions as well, no doubt blurring their focus.

Increasing Violence

With the *de facto* withdrawal of a formal military presence on the frontier, the balance of power seemed once again to favor the Plains Indians. Several bands of Comanches, Kiowas, and others saw the opportunity to strike back at their sworn enemies and to exact vengeance for losses they had incurred. As a result, while the Civil War ground on, the frontier witnessed a significant increase in Indian attacks on settlers and raids against their homesteads and possessions. These resourceful Texans, on the other hand, realized that they were on their own and banded together to provide for their defense.

By 1864 the frontier had become an extremely dangerous place with few zones of safety. Undaunted, Palo Pinto County cattleman Charles Goodnight, recently discharged from the Frontier Regiment, attempted to rebuild his scattered fortune and drove a herd of cattle from his ranch to a new range on Elm Creek in Young County. After seeing his cattle safe to their new pastures in July, he threw in with the inhabitants of some fortified cabins known as Fort Murrah (or Murray). That night, his brother-in-law and partner Alfred Lane had a dream that Indians massacred his parents back in Palo Pinto County. Despite all of Goodnight's warnings and concerns, Lane decided to head back home on his own to check on the fate of his people.

Lane set off to his doom. After traveling only eight or ten miles across the Elm Creek prairie, he was surprised by a band of Comanche and Kiowa warriors. They easily overran him and then tortured him to death, scalping and mutilating his corpse. His parents, on the other hand, remained safe on their ranch in Palo Pinto County. This chance encounter served as an opening act in an Indian offensive that would come later that year.

The Cox Mountain Fight

More trouble was brewing. Comanche and Kiowa warriors grew increasingly bold, banding together in larger numbers and wreaking havoc on isolated settlers, often within sight of the abandoned buildings of the old U.S. forts. The militia of the Frontier Organization attempted a response, but they were facing much stronger opposition than before.

On August 9, between present-day Cisco and Eastland, a group of eight militiamen under the command of Corporal James Head discovered the trail of a sizable group of Indians and dutifully tracked the warriors as they headed south toward the settlements of Eastland County. Near present-day Gorman the patrol drew up on a sight that shocked them: nearly fifty well-armed Comanches and Kiowas bent on mischief, many of whom were dismounted and obviously hunting for horses. The militiamen rode a few miles to the perceived safety of Lieutenant Singleton Gilbert's Ranch cabin near Ellison Springs while alerting the rest of the militia of the situation. Before long, sixteen Texans had gathered to contest this Indian raid.

The Texans decided that audacity would carry the day. Figuring that they had the advantage, Lieutenant Gilbert and his squad closed in on the Indians and launched a mounted charge, hoping to surprise the warriors and overrun those on foot. Instead, the natives wheeled around and unleashed bullets and arrows, emptying three Texan saddles. Gilbert was among the dead. The militiamen turned and fled, carrying three wounded with them. The Indians continued on with their horse-stealing mission with the Texans keeping their distance.

The Indians had won that round but would not remain unscathed. Scores of horses disappeared throughout the area, but an eight-man patrol of militiamen in Stephens

County under Sergeant A.D. Miller picked up some of the raiders' trail as they headed back toward the Red River. After tracking these twenty Comanches and Kiowa for a dozen miles, Miller's men launched into them, inaugurating a one-hour gun battle. The Indians escaped, but they lost two of their number and seventy-three of the horses they had stolen.

These once routine patrols, which often had served double duty as cow hunts for these citizens-turned-soldiers, had taken an ominous turn. The larger size of the Indian raiding parties and the recent haul of horses indicated to many on the frontier signs that a major escalation was occurring. Even so, some figured the benefits of pioneering in this cattleman's paradise was worth the risk. On the thirteenth of September, five Young County men headed into Lost Valley in neighboring Jack County for the annual roundup of their herds. The group included William R. Peveler, Captain of the Young County Militia, and State Cox, Sheriff of Young County.

As they made their way back home, traveling through an area about ten miles north of present-day Graham, they spotted about ten Comanches in the distance. The men decided to kill these raiders while they could and spurred their horses toward the Indians, following them into a dense mesquite thicket. Once in the thicket, the Texans realized that they had made a terrible mistake and could discern some fifty Comanche and Kiowa warriors in ambush. To make matters worse for the cow men, Cox's horse had gone lame in the charge and was now limping.

Outnumbered, the men decided to dismount and share Cox's fate, but the sheriff refused to allow his friends and neighbors to do so, pleading with them to save themselves. The men reluctantly gave in to his entreaties and Militia Captain Peveler ordered a full retreat. Cox, thinking to make the best of terrible situation, also mounted his horse and spurred it forward; in his excitement he had failed to untie it from a tree. The horse jumped forward, the rope went taut, and snapped its neck. Cox fell to the ground badly injured. The Indians knew they had been discovered and filled Cox with arrows, killing him quickly.

Peveler and the other men raced out of the thicket, but the captain and his horse took several arrows in the initial volley, slowing him down considerably. As the others hurried away from him toward Fort Belknap, Peveler was only able to make it a few hundred yards more to a deep ravine. There was only one path through the ravine, traversing steep walls on both sides. Peveler's wounded horse plunged into the gully and climbed the far wall as several warriors headed down into the ravine behind him. Peveler turned in his saddle and fired his pistol at the first Indian, killing him instantly. The other Indian mounts shied and Peveler escaped. Badly wounded, he traveled with an arrow sticking out of his neck to a settler's house. The neighbor removed the arrow with great difficulty and then discovered that Peveler had fifteen other wounds throughout his body. The militia captain died fifteen days later.

The incident was quite disturbing to settlers, especially in Young County. To have fifty or sixty warriors prowling was

cause enough for alarm, but to have to bury two of their leading citizens added bitterness to their plight. The residents of
the area came to call the hill near the deadly mesquite thicket Cox Mountain, and most hoped to avoid lending their
name posthumously to some feature in this troubled land.
Their suffering, however, had just begun.

The Elm Creek Raid

In western Young County, residents built a prosperous
existence in the safe shadow of Fort Belknap and on the route
of the Butterfield Overland Mail. For many, their lives were
infinitely better than they would have been in a more settled
area. One of the most interesting and important residents
would end her life as Elizabeth Ann Carter FitzPatrick
Clifton. Born in Alabama in 1825, she was married at age sixteen to Alexander Joseph Carter, a free black man. The
Carters, who had two children, moved to Texas and eventually settled west of Fort Belknap and started a ranch. Elizabeth
managed the ranch, a boarding house, and a mercantile operation all known as the Carter Trading House. Her husband
and father-in-law ran a freighting business, but in 1857 they
were murdered. Despite this tragedy, Elizabeth continued to
manage the ranch and the Trading House with great efficiency and success. In 1862 she married one of the ranch hands,
Thomas FitzPatrick. Tragically, he was murdered eighteen
months later.

Shortly afterward, fate would compound her misery. On
October 13, 1864, a party of some two hundred Comanche and

Kiowa Indians, a huge force by the standards of frontier warfare, launched a raid of plundering and retaliation along Elm Creek. They were aided, survivors reported, by at least one white—perhaps a captive who had grown up in the tribe or a simple brigand. Their first attack was on the home of Peter Harmonson, who saw the Indians coming, and he escaped with his son Perry, who had nearly been killed with Cox and Peveler a month before. The two dismounted and took cover in some timber nearby, prepared to sell their lives dearly. When the Indians tried to follow them, Harmonson shot one, dressed in a U.S. army jacket, off of his horse, discouraging the others from continuing the hunt. The Harmonsons fled, spreading the alarm to other ranches as they headed for Fort Murrah.

Knowing that the settlers could do little to resist, the Indians loitered in the area, divided into smaller raiding parties, and systematically went from ranch to ranch destroying or stealing property. One group moved to the next dwelling along the creek—the Carter Trading House, which was full of people that day. Elizabeth FitzPatrick was home with her thirteen-year-old son Joe and her married daughter, Mildred Susanna Carter Durkin. Also present on the ranch were Elizabeth's three grandchildren: two young girls, Millie and Lottie Durkin, and an infant boy. Elizabeth was also hosting Mary Johnson, a slave woman from the nearby ranch of Moses Johnson, and her two young daughters and infant son while her husband, Britton, was away.

The Indians attacked the Carter Trading House swiftly and with complete surprise. They first killed Elizabeth's

Elizabeth Carter Clifton as portrayed at Frontier Texas

daughter Mildred and her infant son, then turned on the Johnson infant. Having killed those that might impede their progress, the Indians took captive Elizabeth, her son, and her two surviving granddaughters, along with Mary Johnson and her two daughters.

By now the other residents along Elm Creek had become aware of the threat. Most fled their homes, figuring that hiding among the cedar breaks or along the cliffs of the Brazos was safer. Dr. Thomas Wilson, Thomas Hamby, and his Confederate soldier son, Thornton K. Hamby, rode through the region warning and gathering up families to be prepared to defend themselves against the oncoming Indians. Wilson and the Hambys took the refugees to a fortified cabin owned by George Bragg and set up a defensive position.

This cluster of Texans would be a little more challenging for the Indians. One band arrived and made several bold rides around the cabin, killing Wilson as he attempted to shoot back. After a few more exchanges, Bragg collapsed with an arrow in his chest while the elder Hamby recoiled with two gunshots to his shoulder. With only one able defender left, the families inside faced an uncertain future. One Indian dismounted, picked up a mattock from the yard, and began hammering against the outside wall of the cabin, determined to form a breech. As the nine women and children cowered behind furniture and beneath the bed, Thornton Hamby edged the barrel of his pistol through the growing crack, and put a bullet into the Indian's head.

Some dismounted, settling on a siege while the majority rode away to investigate a growing battle nearby. Those Indians who remained continued assaults on the cabin until nightfall, when they rode away never having entered the dwelling.

In the meantime a serious fight had developed between a small squad from Company D of the Border Regiment and some of the more scattered Indians. While on routine patrol the Confederates killed two dismounted Indians ransacking a ranch, but the sound of gunfire drew them away from this minor encounter. Soon they found themselves engaging larger and larger numbers of Comanches and Kiowas—several hundred well-armed and well-mounted Indians. The squad's commander, Lt. Nathan F. Carson, ordered his men to regroup, form a line of battle, and make a fighting withdrawal.

The soldiers did not panic and made a skillful fight of it. "I ordered my men to fall back some 100 yards to gain a better position, in slow order, to save the men that were on weak horses," reported Carson, "fighting them from one position to another until five of my brave men were killed." Several of the troops had been hit, and the Lieutenant took two minor hits as well, but reported that his men killed at least seven and undoubtedly wounded others. His shot up command fell back onto the McCoy Ranch and saved two women, his soldiers pulling them onto their horses. The soldiers rode away toward the group of cabins settlers called Fort Murrah, picking up an additional six men from their command along the way. Some Indians half-heartedly pursued while others paused to plunder the dead, pick off stray settlers, and ransack ranches.

Elsewhere, pioneers died alone on the prairie. Joel Myers, apparently unaware of the gravity of his situation, tried to drive a pair of oxen to safety near the mouth of Elm Creek. Indians surrounded him, killed and mutilated him, then added his scalp to the days' trophies. James McCoy and his son Miles were also dead, surprised by Indians while splitting rails for a fence.

Henry Wooten, also alone on the prairie, made a dash for Fort Belknap in hopes of finding soldiers there. Several Indians spotted him whipping his pony across the plain and immediately pursued. A skillful shot dropped the pioneer's horse. Afoot and outnumbered, he continued his flight. As Indians closed on him, Wooten turned and threatened them with a pistol, causing them to veer off. Deciding not to bother with this scrappy white man, the Indians instead scalped the man's horse, removing mane and ears, and topped the unusual pelt with Wooten's hat, mocking the scared man and hastening his retreat.

The raid had devastated the area. At Fort Murrah, thirty-five armed citizens and soldiers protected several dozen families, the women and children filling buckets with water and stockpiling ammunition for one final stand. On the roof of one of the cabins, a settler with a telescope claimed he counted 375 Indians moving across the prairie. No one there had seen anything like it. Instead of finishing off the little pockets of resistance at the Bragg cabin and at Fort Murrah, the Indians set fire to the prairie, burned anything else they could to keep the settlers guessing, and then headed home, counting among their gains dozens of stolen horses, hundreds of cattle, and their captives from the Carter Trading House. Behind them smoke from a dozen burning cabins snaked into the sky, and sixteen settlers and soldiers lay dead.

The Elm Creek Raid had several consequences. Frontier settlers were unnerved by the boldness of the assault, and the relatively large number of Indians involved and captives taken. The county militias, and state and Confederate authorities vowed to become more aggressive in policing and patrolling the frontier. For the white residents there, gone were the days of cow hunts and hopeful futures. Now they merely hoped to make it to the springtime alive.

Fate of the Elm Creek Captives

When the Elm Creek raiders left the region, they did so with seven captives in tow. By the second day of traveling, however, they decided that Elizabeth FitzPatrick's thirteen-year-old son was too much trouble, so they killed him and left his body on the trail. The other captives, including FitzPatrick and her two granddaughters, and Mary Johnson and her two daughters, were then divided up among the different bands and tribes that made up the raiding party.

FitzPatrick ended up in the custody of Kiowa chief Sun Boy. She was taken to his camp on the Arkansas River in northwestern Kansas. Her granddaughters ended up in two different Comanche camps. Two-year-old Millie, along with several other captive children, froze to death that winter at Comanche Chief Iron Mountain's camp. Five-year-old Lottie, on the other hand, remained in Comanche hands for nine months, until they finally released her back to her home. They left her with a permanent reminder of her captivity—they tattooed her arms and forehead before they released her.

Troops under the command of Gen. J.H. Leavenworth finally rescued Elizabeth FitzPatrick, twelve months and twenty days after her capture. They took her to the Kaw Mission at Council Grove, Kansas, where she earned three dollars a week to nurse and care for other recently released captives. She finally returned to Texas in August of 1866, nearly two years after the Elm Creek Raid. Reunited with her granddaughter Lottie, Elizabeth moved on with her life, marrying Parker County widower Isaac Clifton in 1869. She never gave up hope that her other granddaughter, Millie, would be found alive, but this was not to be. Elizabeth died in 1882 at Fort Griffin.

Mary Johnson and her two children also gained release, but through much more intriguing circumstances. Her husband, Britton, had been away buying supplies at the time of the Elm Creek Raid, but he was a man of extraordinary drive and determination. Britt was born a slave in Tennessee in 1840. He came to Texas in the 1850s with his master Moses Johnson, who had bought land along Elm Creek. As a reward for Britt's loyalty and hard work, Moses Johnson appointed

Britt Johnson as portrayed at Frontier Texas

Asa Havey as portrayed at Frontier Texas

him foreman of the ranch, with unlimited freedom to perform his duties. He also permitted Britt to raise his own horses and cattle.

When the Elm Creek Raid took his son's life and the liberty of his wife and daughters, Britt Johnson's life changed drastically. His attempts to find his family became the source of legend. He asked his owner for permission to leave; Moses Johnson not only granted it, but he sent Britt off with half of all of his money. For several months after the Elm Creek Raid, Britt traveled to numerous reservations in Indian Territory and to forts throughout the Texas frontier, desperate to find his family. Popular tradition claims that Johnson lived with the Comanches in the Spring of 1865 and was able to ransom his family through this connection. The rescue of the Johnsons, however, actually came as part of ongoing peace negotiations and the efforts of friendly Comanches. In June 1865 Penateka Comanche Chief Asa Havey paid a ransom for the captives, rescued them, and took them to the Indian agent, who turned them over to Johnson.

By the time Johnson returned with his family, the Civil War was over and he was a free man. He had become famous on the frontier, and he used his status to buy a wagon team and gain freight contracts after the war. He moved his family to Parker County, where he headquartered his freight business. Johnson became quite successful, heading up wagon teams to haul freight between Weatherford and Fort Griffin.

Citizen Forts and the Battle of Dove Creek

Throughout the frontier borderland, settlers reacted to the Elm Creek Raid. The people of the Northwest Texas Frontier, still counting their losses from the Elm Creek Raid—or still hearing the stories, second and third hand—began thinking defensively. Fort Murrah and the defense of the Bragg Cabin taught them that the time had come to "fort up" and look to their friends and neighbors for mutual protection.

By congregating together in a specific area for mutual protection, those who "forted up" felt that safety from future raids would only be available if they met the Indians in significant numbers from defensible positions. Numerous citizen forts sprang up on the frontier, sporting names such as Fort Hubbard, Fort Clark, and Fort Owl Head.

One of the most famous citizen forts was Fort Davis in Stephens County. Established only three weeks after the Elm Creek Raid, this fort typified the type of defensive settlement that formed during the war. It measured about 300 by 325 feet and housed approximately 125 people from twenty-five families. The compound divided into sixteen seventy-five-square-foot lots, divided by streets and alleys, with one main street running east-west through the center. The settlers constructed all of their houses from pickets daubed with mud, but the fort had been built around an earlier stone house in which women and children could retreat in case of Indian attack. Supplies had to be freighted in from the eastern part of the state—always an extremely dangerous journey.

Another major consequence of the Elm Creek Raid was an increased aggressiveness by frontier military groups. Local militias increased patrols while state and Confederate troops remained at the ready at the first sign of Indian activity. It was in this state of hyper-attentiveness that the largest battle with Indians during the Civil War occurred.

In December of 1864, Capt. N.M. Gillintine led a militia scouting party of twenty-three from the Second Frontier District along the Clear Fork of the Brazos. The party moved north to the ruins of Fort Phantom Hill, then continued up the river where, on December 9, they discovered an abandoned Indian camp about thirty miles past the old fort. Gillintine reported ninety-two lodge sites at the camp, causing great alarm among residents of the frontier counties, as a camp this size could have housed at least one hundred warriors. Gillintine's command returned without finding where the Indians had gone or, as it turned out, identifying who they were. To the people of frontier Texas, any Indian was assumed hostile, especially after Elm Creek.

That many Indians made everyone in the region nervous, and the Texans resolved to find where they had gone and destroy them. Brig. Gen. James McAdoo, commander of the Second and Third Frontier Military Districts, ordered the formation of the largest strike force assembled by the state—325 militiamen from Bosque, Comanche, Coryell, Erath, and Johnson counties under the command of Capt. S. S. Totten. In addition, Capt. Henry Fossett's company from the Frontier Regiment would rendezvous with the column at Fort

Chadbourne. The Confederates arrived first, and after two days of waiting, Fossett grew impatient and ordered his men to set out alone on January 3, 1865.

On January 7, Fossett's scouts spotted the Indian encampment and reported back to their captain that they had found a large Comanche or Kiowa camp numbering some six hundred people. The time to avenge the dead of Elm Creek seemed at hand. Unknown to these Confederate hotspurs, this was in fact a relatively large group of peaceful but determined Kickapoo Indians who had begun a southerly migration toward Mexico in hopes of avoiding the increasingly bloody Texas frontier. This band, a remnant of a once powerful nation from the Great Lakes region, had historically defied all attempts to control them—they simply moved away from trouble when they could in order to maintain their traditional way of life. Trouble had found them on this day as they camped in a timbered area along Dove Creek, near the North Concho River.

Certain that these Indians were in fact some of those responsible for Elm Creek, Fossett fell back and made plans to administer justice. Early the next day, before Fossett could launch his morning assault, Totten's lumbering militia rode into the area on exhausted horses. Fossett and Totten threw together a joint attack plan that involved the militia dismounting and wading across the creek in a frontal assault from the north, while the Confederate troops circled to the southwest, captured the Indian horses, and attacked from the south, cutting off any chance for escape.

The plan fell apart from the beginning. Fossett's mounted Confederates struck first, surprising the Indians guarding the grazing horses. "The Indians were generally in their wigwams," reported one officer. "No fire was made by the Indians until they were fired upon and some of them killed. They showed no disposition to fight." The gunfire set off a panic in the village. "The women were screaming about the camp, some of them in plain English declaring they were friendly." Captain Fossett ordered his men to continue, "saying that he recognized no friendly Indians on the Texas frontier." Meanwhile, Totten's militia stumbled forward as well, delayed by their creek crossing and heavy briars.

The Kickapoos, after determining that the Texans wanted a fight, decided to oblige. Their town was well situated on higher ground west of the creek in a heavy thicket, offering defensive cover and good fields of fire. In the first few minutes of the fight, Kickapoo riflemen cut Totten's troops to pieces, killing nineteen of the luckless militiamen, including Captain Gillintine, and wounding at least a dozen. The rest of these inexperienced men broke and ran, splashing back across Dove Creek and out of the fight.

The soldiers from the Frontier Regiment were all alone. By now, Captain Fossett's mounted Confederates had successfully captured the Indian horses. He ordered Lt. J.A. Brooks to close the trap and to advance with seventy-five men on the Indian town from the south. The Kickapoos, having shifted their attention from the north side of their camp, met this attack with equal enthusiasm, killing twelve horses as they broke up the Confederate attack. Stunned, the Texans dismounted and went to ground in three isolated pockets, dazed by this turn of events. By nightfall, the Kickapoos had recaptured their horses and Fossett's men limped away, fearful of an Indian counterattack.

Both sides were shocked by this battle. The humiliated Confederates and Texas militia rallied several miles away at Spring Creek, but spent a miserable night as rain turned to snow. They remained in the field the entire next day, some butchering their wounded horses for food. They gathered their own wounded and retreated eastward on January 11, finding shelter at John Chisum's Ranch at the confluence of the Concho and Colorado Rivers. Many of the militia, however, did not stop until they reached their homes. This battle would have long-lasting effects on the Kickapoo as well. This tribe had been relatively peaceful on the Texas frontier, but the Dove Creek battle not only killed fourteen of them, but it embittered them against the Texans. They continued their move to the Mexican state of Coahuila but began a vengeful border war of their own against white settlers along the Rio Grande.

Life in the Citizen Forts

The state's great Indian offensive at Dove Creek was a disaster by all accounts. It targeted the wrong Indians at the wrong place and did it poorly. For the settlers in Northwest Texas, however, life in the citizen forts brought some unexpected benefits. It brought to these settlers a sense of community. Before the war, the overwhelming majority of them

Oil on canvas, Accession # 1981.152. Gift of Reilly Nail and Matilda Nail Peeler, from the Collection of the Old Jail Art Center, Albany, Texas.

Presenting the Flag, Fort Davis by Alice Reynolds, 1941

had led fairly isolated lives on the cattle frontier, living as small family units and visiting others only rarely. For women and children especially, this close contact filled a void in their lives. At Fort Davis settlers built a school house and commenced regular school lessons for the children. They also organized a Sunday School, where they read from a Bible and had community discussions about its meaning.

Fort residents also used the sense of community to provide for their basic needs. At Fort Davis, there was a community milk pen where the women would gather to milk the cows. The men usually sat on the fence around the perimeter of the fort, armed and watching for Indians. Women also spent considerable time carding, spinning, weaving cloth, and making candles. They also used lye leached from wood ashes to make soap. Food was still plentiful, as there were fish in nearby streams and deer, antelope, and buffalo still in abundant numbers throughout the region.

Community spirit grew within the confines of these forts. At Fort Davis, they even decided that they needed to make a flag to fly overhead, since they lived in a fort. One of the women volunteered to sew the banner, while others prepared the cords and ropes necessary to fly it. They decided to have a real ceremony in raising the flag, so they invited settlers from Fort Belknap and other area citizen forts to attend. Held on March 2, 1865, the event included band music, speeches, and a dance held in the school house.

Despite the danger that still lurked in the area, settlers at Fort Davis made the most of their time together. They had weddings and square dances, quilting parties and candy pulls. One of the favorite activities for the younger residents of the fort was dancing. There were many fiddlers among the settlers, and they would often play well into the night. On one occasion, several young men from neighboring ranches arrived for a dance at the fort. They tied their horses and went in for an evening of revelry. When the dance ended, the men found that their horses had been taken. Upon further investigation, they discovered that the soft earth on the nearby river bank had been patted down by several moccasined feet. It became evident that a party of Indians had danced to the fiddle music themselves before taking all of the horses.

Born out of the violence of frontier warfare, the community atmosphere of these citizen forts inadvertently created a unique oasis experience for these previously isolated settlers on the frontier. The dangers of the unprotected region forced them together, giving a foretaste of what a future West Texas might be. Most of the citizen forts were abandoned even before the Civil War ended. By 1867 U.S. military presence had returned to the region, and settlers could return to their more isolated cattle-raising lives.

Chapter Five
The Military Returns to the Frontier, 1865-1880

By the end of the Civil War, the Texas frontier was as much a borderland as ever. Confederate troops had dissolved along with the nation they represented, and state troops and militia organized during the war stayed home. Under the terms of Reconstruction the Texas frontier sat bereft of armed protection just at a time when the Indians had become emboldened. The U.S. Army had not yet returned to its posts as it slowly shifted from being a modern juggernaut to a frontier constabulary. In this strange military twilight settlers in the region once again turned to their own resources to protect themselves and their families from Indian raids.

In 1866 John Eubank of Shackelford County was ready to move forward with life. He and his family lived near a few other settlers, and they all planned to round up their cattle jointly for mutual protection from Indian attacks. The Shackelford County stock hunters set a time and place to rendezvous about ten miles from the Eubank Ranch, and Eubank sent his teenaged son, Thomas, armed only with a pistol, to meet them.

A few weeks later the stockmen returned from the roundup and Eubank greeted them to find out their success.

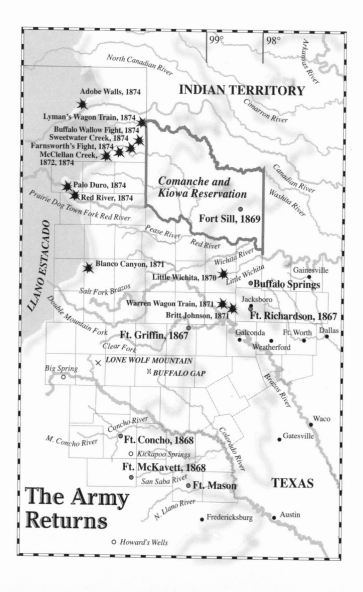

Adobe Walls, 1874

INDIAN TERRITORY

Lyman's Wagon Train, 1874
Buffalo Wallow Fight, 1874
Sweetwater Creek, 1874
Farnsworth's Fight, 1874
McClellan Creek, 1872, 1874

Palo Duro, 1874
Red River, 1874

North Canadian River

Arkansas River

Cimarron River

Canadian River

Washita River

Comanche and Kiowa Reservation

Fort Sill, 1869

Prairie Dog Town Fork Red River

LLANO ESTACADO

Pease River

Red River

Blanco Canyon, 1871

Little Wichita, 1870

Wichita River

Little Wichita

Gainesville

Salt Fork Brazos

Buffalo Springs

Double Mountain Fork

Warren Wagon Train, 1871
Britt Johnson, 1871

Jacksboro

Ft. Richardson, 1867

Ft. Griffin, 1867

Galconda

Ft. Worth

Dallas

Clear Fork

LONE WOLF MOUNTAIN

Weatherford

Big Spring

)(*BUFFALO GAP*

Brazos River

Waco

Concho River

M. Concho River

Ft. Concho, 1868

Gatesville

Kickapoo Springs

Colorado River

Ft. McKavett, 1868

San Saba River

Ft. Mason

TEXAS

The Army Returns

N. Llano River

Fredericksburg

Austin

Howard's Wells

Only then did he discover that his son had never joined the hunt. Several men immediately started a search party along the road to the rendezvous. Along the trail they came across the carcasses of two horses that had been killed with pistol bullets. They continued the search and rode to the top of some nearby rugged terrain. Once there, a strong odor overwhelmed their senses, and they found hidden in the brush the corpse of a dead Indian. The man had also been killed by a pistol shot and was wrapped in a blanket, tied with a belt that Eubank identified as having belonged to his son.

Finding no other evidence of his son's presence, Eubank felt sure that Thomas had been captured. He tried to contact government officials for help in ascertaining his son's whereabouts, but to no avail. A few weeks later, some boys were hunting cattle on the same prairie where the two dead horses had been found, and they came across a skeleton. On the skeleton were items that conclusively identified it as the corpse of Thomas Eubank.

A lonely death on the prairie, more than anything else, unsettled the early pioneers of frontier Texas and they eagerly sought some assistance from any quarter in order to improve their odds. The presence of U.S. military garrisons had been among the factors luring them to the region, and these citizens demanded that the government once again provide some means of protection. Texas Provisional Governor A.J. Hamilton received countless petitions pleading for a return of the military to the region. By 1866, however, the governor was bound by the control of Congressional

Reconstruction. Texas had been made a military district under martial law, so Hamilton sent requests through official channels to the district commander, Gen. H.G. Wright, for cavalry to patrol the frontier region. Wright deferred the issue, claiming no authority over the cavalry. The request then went to Gen. Phil Sheridan, Commander of the Division of the Southwest, but Sheridan responded that all cavalry units had to remain in the interior to protect the recently freed slaves. Until Washington could develop a new plan for frontier defense, the settlers were on their own.

Return of the Frontier Forts

The U.S. Army eventually addressed the issue of frontier defense. In 1866 the War Department reasserted a policy to recreate the frontier line of forts. The plan was to refurbish some of the pre-Civil War forts, and, where necessary, build new ones to aid in containing the Indian threat. Frontier Texas residents had to wait a year and a half for the blue coats to arrive. When they did the first area in the region to receive attention was Jack County, the site of several Indian raids over the previous few years.

What emerged from this policy was the creation of a third generation of forts in Texas. Elements of the Sixth Cavalry arrived in the fall of 1866 and camped outside of town on Lost Creek while scouting a location for a permanent post. Early in 1867 a detachment moved north a few dozen miles to Buffalo Springs in Clay County but eventually returned because of supply, wood, and water issues. Another portion of the regiment moved to reactivate Fort Belknap in Young County. Their stay, however, was also short-lived. Three months later the War Department decided the force could better serve to protect the frontier farther north in Shackelford County. In July Lt. Col. Samuel D. Sturgis led four companies of the Sixth Cavalry in building Camp Wilson on the Clear Fork of the Brazos River in Shackelford County, not far from the ruins of Camp Cooper. They soon renamed the post Fort Griffin in honor of Gen. Charles Griffin, commander of the Military District of Texas. Fort Belknap remained abandoned, but would serve from that point on as a sub-post. Early the next year, the headquarters of the Sixth Cavalry formalized its camps on Lost Creek into Fort Jacksboro, soon renamed Fort Richardson in honor of Gen. Israel B. Richardson, who had been killed in the Civil War battle of Antietam. Both Fort Griffin and Fort Richardson became active quickly because of their proximity to Indian Territory.

A similar situation played out all along the frontier. Farther south elements of the Fourth Cavalry reactivated Fort Chadbourne in the summer of 1867 but soon discovered that the water supply from Oak Creek was inadequate for their long-term needs. The War Department instead ordered the creation of a new post, Fort Concho, near the confluence of the South, Middle, and North Concho Rivers several dozen miles south of Fort Chadbourne. The old fort, like its contemporary Fort Belknap, became relegated to that of a sub-post, only occasionally occupied and very rarely maintained.

In 1868 troopers and contractors began construction of Fort Concho. The first and most important buildings—the commissary storehouse and the quartermaster storehouse—went up fastest, but the other buildings would take much longer as teamsters hauled material from depots on the Gulf Coast. Nevertheless, by the early 1870s the fort boasted more than forty permanent structures built of quarried limestone, including barracks, stables and blacksmith shops, an ordinance storehouse, a guardhouse, a bakery, a hospital, and a schoolhouse that was also used as a chapel. All of these buildings surrounded a large parade ground that measured about 500 by 1,000 feet. Nearby, a "scabtown" of private businesses and merchants catering to the needs of the soldiers blossomed, calling itself Saint Angela but later slurred into San Angelo.

Meanwhile, the line continued when the War Department decided to reactivate Fort McKavett in 1868. The fort's new commander was Col. Ranald Mackenzie, who was determined to rebuild the post to its former glory. Under his direction, the troops lived in tents for two years as they reconstructed the fort. When they finished, Fort McKavett included four barracks, twelve officers' quarters, a magazine, a hospital, a guardhouse, a bakery, two storehouses, a post office, a headquarters building, a forage house, and a thirty-acre garden.

One other pre-Civil War fort in the region found life in the new era. Headquarters Company with field staff and officers and the regimental band and Company F of the Fourth Cavalry moved into Fort Mason in December 1866. Under the command of Gen. John Porter Hatch, the men had a formidable task in rebuilding the fort and curbing the violence and lawlessness of the region. Using both civilian artisans and military labor, Hatch worked to restore the buildings. His command, however, failed to be effective as many of his men deserted or faced courts–martial for a variety of offenses. Within the next two years, the War Department decided to replace the cavalry forces with soldiers of the Thirty-fifth Infantry. By 1869, however, the fort consisted of twenty-five buildings in various states of disrepair, and it boasted only sixty-nine personnel. In March of that year the War Department decided to close the fort.

The post did have one last brief reprieve in September 1870. When the State of Texas renewed its efforts to field an armed auxiliary to police the frontier, Fort Mason became the headquarters of Companies A and B of the Texas Frontier Forces. Only one short year later, however, the state disbanded these companies and abandoned the fort for the last time. The local citizens moved in and used most of the remaining building material to construct homes of their own.

Most Texans initially hailed the return of the troops enthusiastically, but many tempered this euphoria with feelings of distrust. Some of the new units were composed of African-American troops, many of whom were recently slaves. Some considered this to be a calculated offense by a vindictive government intent upon making an example of the recently defeated South and, by association, Texas. Others could not believe that black men could handle the rugged requirements of the job. Whether these claims were real or imagined, racial friction became commonplace on the Texas frontier as these soldiers took their place, ready to protect settlers, grateful or not. Soon these so-called Buffalo Soldiers earned an enviable reputation as steadfast soldiers, capable fighters, and resourceful campaigners. In addition, they, like white soldiers in other units, helped survey roads, escort the mail, string telegraph lines, and enforce the law. Soldiers, white and black, helped build West Texas.

Failure of the Peace

While the U.S. Army was rebuilding and restaffing the Texas frontier forts, President Andrew Johnson's government was busy trying to establish a more permanent solution to the continued conflicts with Plains Indians. In the spring of 1866, the U.S. Congress established a Peace Commission and charged it with securing agreements with all the western tribes. In October 1867 commissioners called for a major council of Plains Indian tribes to meet on the Medicine Lodge River in Kansas. Between five and seven thousand Indians from the Comanche, Kiowa, Apache, Cheyenne, and Arapahoe nations gathered at the site to negotiate with the government.

The commissioners sought two major concessions from the Indians—land and peace. They persuaded the different tribes to sign the Medicine Lodge Treaty, transferring claim to about 90 million acres of land to the U.S. government in exchange for a firm title to 2.9 million acres on reservations in Indian Territory. The Comanches, Kiowas, and Kiowa Apaches received a grant to a reservation in western Indian Territory from the 98th Meridian west to the 100th Meridian, and from the Red River north to the Washita River. The government also promised to provide the tribes with a variety of support on the reservations, including buildings, physicians, farming instructors, and schools. The Indians, in turn, were to remain on the reservations, leaving the frontier areas available to settlement without interference. The Indians did retain the right to hunt buffalo, according to the treaty, "on any lands south of the Arkansas River so long as the buffalo may range thereon," but only by permit from authorities.

This new order would be swiftly implemented. The government allowed the Indians a few months to move to their new homes but moved quickly to snuff out resistance. Authorities would use the U.S. Army to shepherd those who hesitated or resisted. In the fall of 1868 elements of six different regiments, some two thousand men, launched a massive military sweep of the region, overrunning several Indian encampments and aggressively pursuing so-called "holdouts." The campaign had its desired effect, and the final, demoralized Indians of the southern Great Plains moved into their new accommodations. As an experimental component of this new policy, the administration of recently elected President Ulysses S. Grant assigned agents—all of whom were Quaker pacifists—to conduct the official business of the various tribes. The Army moved once again into the role of peacekeeper.

A symbol of this new regime soon emerged. In January 1869, Gen. Phil Sheridan established Camp Washita, later named Fort Sill after his West Point roommate, Joshua Sill, killed at Stone's River in the Civil War. Designed to project power and to serve as a trading post for the new reservations, this facility became the most important in the region. Government agents, licensed traders, and contractors all headquartered nearby, eager to implement the various terms of the Medicine Lodge Treaty and make a profit if they could. Despite this great attempt at social engineering, these same government appointees would earn a reputation for corruption, graft, inefficiency, and incompetence.

U.S. government officials put great hope in the Medicine Lodge Treaty, but settlers on the frontier saw little change in the dangers of the region. Many Comanche and Kiowa chiefs, having been forced to abide by the treaty, sulked at this humiliation. Other refused to recognize its legitimacy because they had not been present at the negotiations. Others claimed that white settlers and cattlemen were still using land set aside for their reservation or for their hunts, and the excesses of government appointees fell hard on these once proud people. Soon, in small groups and then much larger, Indians slipped away from the reservation to taste again the freedom of the plains. Some used their hunting passes to justify their departure. Others simply left for the adventure without permission. Along the Texas frontier, the sporadic raids and killings that white settlers had coped with for years continued.

Increasingly, the Kiowas became a major player in this drama. Originally from the northern Great Plains near the Yellowstone River and western Montana, these relatives of the Crow Indians drifted south to the Arkansas River in the late 1700s and early 1800s, picking up a small, unrelated band of a few hundred Plains Apaches along the way. By the 1790s, the Kiowas and Kiowa-Apaches had joined into a lasting alliance with the Comanches. Unlike their new associates, the Kiowas followed a simple tribal organization with a principal chief who dictated, with advice, the course of his nation. Deeply religious, the Kiowas conducted an annual Sun Dance every summer to renew tribal unity and strength and believed in the power of a collection of sacred bundles, known as the ten grandmothers, to keep them safe. By the 1840s the Kiowas, never more than two thousand strong, added the Southern Cheyennes and Arapahos to their list of allies. For the next twenty-five years the Kiowas prospered, enjoying reasonably good relations with the United States while making occasional forays along with their more numerous and powerful Comanche allies into Texas and Mexico.

The late 1860s visited a variety of calamities on the Kiowas. Unlike the Comanches and their loosely organized and widely scattered bands, the Kiowas had always been fairly cohesive and had followed the leadership of Dohësan, or Little Mountain, as their principal chief since 1832. In 1866 this great unifying leader died, unleashing a power struggle that sundered their society. Tribal leaders recognized Guipago, or Lone Wolf, as the new principal chief, but his unyielding militancy put him at odds with most Kiowas.

The Medicine Lodge Treaty exacerbated the tribal split. The forced removal to a reservation south of their homes of the last fifty years pitted those who would accept a negotiated peace with the whites against those who were irreconcilable. Each rival sought new ways to gain prestige and a following; raiding the frontier and defying U.S. authority was a tested way to prove one's mettle. As a result, many Kiowas began seeking to demonstrate their prowess in

Photograph by William S. Soule, 1868-1874. National Archives and Records Administration

Lone Wolf

battle. In opposition to this trend, Tene-Angopte, or Kicking Bird, advocated cooperation with U.S. authorities and knew that a new, if unpleasant, age had dawned for his people. As conditions on the reservation worsened, he bore much of his people's hostility, fueled by his rival and leader of the war faction, Lone Wolf, and his young protégé, twenty-year-old Ado-Eete or Big Tree. Meanwhile, seventy-year-old medicine man Satank—Sitting Bear in English—and fifty-year-old Satanta, also known as White Bear, began to have second thoughts even after signing the treaty. As members of the elite *Koitsenko* warrior society, these old veterans had pledged to protect the

Photograph by William S. Soule, 1868-1874. National Archives and Records Administration

Satank

tribe. For them, the question remained as how best to do that.

The confusion among the Kiowas even extended to the spiritual realm. Perhaps the most dangerous of the emerging Kiowa leadership was a thirty-five-year-old shaman called Maman-Ti, or Sky Walker. This mystic claimed supernatural powers, including powerful visions and the ability to communicate with the dead. After the death of Little Mountain, this brooding upstart adopted the role of a Kiowa *dohate,* or Owl Prophet. He evangelized his fellow Kiowas on the need to kill soldiers and settlers as a way to get right with the cosmos, and he blessed many expeditions of young men crossing the Red River to answer his evangelist's call. He even led a few himself. His rival was Zepko-ette, or Big Bow, a spiritual skeptic who also advocated war but relied on his own strength and courage for salvation. Scornful of what he considered to be his people's superstitions, Big Bow mostly lived apart from the Kiowas and felt more at home with the Quahadi Comanches. He and his friend and contemporary Tsent-Tainte, or White Horse, earned notoriety as being among the most ferocious of the Kiowa war leaders.

Before long, the Kiowas and their mélange of competing leaders rivaled in reputation their Comanche allies for spreading dread and mayhem on the Texas frontier. They were swift and fearless and would not hesitate to wrangle even with tough and well-armed opponents. During the summer of 1870 the war faction even stampeded the middle-aged Kicking Bird, the most pro-American of the Kiowa leadership, into leading a raid to prove his bravery and worthiness as a leader. When young men in his 100-

Photograph by William S. Soule, 1868-1874. National Archives and Records Administration

Satanta

warrior party sacked a mail station in Jack County, U.S. troops from the Sixth Cavalry at Fort Richardson responded.

The two parties met at the Little Wichita River. On July 11 a civilian scout reported to Capt. Curwen B. McLellan that the Indians were encamped along the banks of that stream. The next morning he ordered a mounted charge through the town. The intensity of the Indian defense astounded him, and he quickly realized that he was outnumbered and, more importantly, out-gunned. The Kiowas had a sizable number of Spencer repeating rifles on hand, and their sustained fire disorganized the U.S. troops. At that point, Kicking Bird ordered a counter-attack, personally dispatching one corporal with his lance. The soldiers reeled under this assault and fell back, leaving three dead on the field.

The battle lasted all day as the troopers continued to retreat under pressure from Kicking Bird's Kiowas. By nightfall McLellan's men, carrying eleven wounded with them, had withdrawn nearly twenty miles while in constant combat with the Indians. After spending a nervous night, the cavalrymen burned their baggage and made their way to a fortified position until rescued by reinforcements. Unwittingly, McLellan gave the Kiowa leader what he had come seeking, remarking on the chief's superior generalship during the course of the long day's battle. Kicking Bird returned to the reservation with the admiration of his people and the respect of his enemies and once again took up the cause of peace.

For makers of Indian policy as well as the citizens who would benefit or suffer from it, this sort of behavior appeared bewildering. The one thing the settlers of the Texas frontier were convinced of, though, was that the Comanches and their Kiowa allies were using the Fort Sill Reservation as a safe haven and source of supplies. Unscrupulous traders happily sold contraband items to the Indians, including repeating firearms. They also gladly purchased horses and other items brought in, no questions asked. Texans suspected that government beef fattened the raiders and that its agents issued them blankets and clothes for the long nights on the trail. While politicians and military commanders assured these anxious citizens that the situation was well in hand, the men and women on isolated ranches and farmsteads had reason to distrust their rosy reports.

Despite this atmosphere of uncertainty, Britt Johnson had reason to be optimistic. Now a free man, he had become a legend among frontier communities after he successfully returned his wife and daughters from Comanche captivity following the Elm Creek Raid. With the reintroduction of U.S. troops to the region, the freed slave was able to build a burgeoning freight business doing jobs for the government. His wagon teams traveled regularly between Weatherford and Forts Richardson and Griffin, hauling supplies and materials for the new garrisons. With an enviable income, his family safe, a heroic reputation, and a growing business, Johnson was becoming one of the major success stories of frontier Texas.

That was until January 24, 1871. While Johnson and two employees worried a string of freight wagons through Young County, a group of twenty-five Kiowas—probably led by Sky Walker himself—attacked his party four miles to the east of Salt Creek. The teamsters made a hasty defense, but two fell from Indian gunfire in the first rush, leaving Johnson alone and outnumbered. There was little cover, but using his dead horse for protection Johnson held back the attack for several more minutes. He apparently died defending this position. When other teamsters found the site of this attack, they counted 173 rifle and pistol shells around the area where Johnson made his stand. The teamsters buried the mutilated bodies of Johnson and his men in a common grave next to the wagon road.

William T. Sherman
and the Warren Wagon Train Raid

Reports of such continued violence on the frontier confounded U.S. government officials. With the Medicine Lodge Treaty, they believed that the major difficulties with Plains Indians on the Texas frontier had been settled. The Quaker Indians agents reported that their charges were taking to their new lives with great abandon. Contractors who distributed rations and other necessaries to the Indians claimed, too, that all was well. Many dismissed the complaints coming from Texas as being overly dramatic and perhaps the inflated whining of citizens who, it was noted, had only recently rebelled against the same government to which they now begged for assistance. To investigate the continuing complaints, Gen. William Tecumseh Sherman, Commanding General of the U.S. Army, decided to travel to Texas in 1871. He accompanied Inspector General Randolph B. Marcy, a veteran of the Texas frontier, in his already scheduled trip to inspect the newly established line of forts.

The pair, accompanied by only a small escort of mounted Buffalo Soldiers, left San Antonio and moved toward the frontier forts to the northwest. They arrived safely in the region and carried out routine inspections on Forts McKavett, Concho, and Chadbourne, passed the ruins of Fort Phantom Hill, and went on to Forts Griffin and Belknap. Sherman continued to believe that reports of Indian violence had been overstated, and he exclaimed, "I have seen not a trace of an Indian thus far and only hear the stories of the people, which indicates that whatever Indians there be only come to Texas to steal horses."

Sherman's unwillingness to believe that the danger was any greater was soon changed by a near brush with disaster. On May 17 Sherman's small entourage left Fort Belknap for Fort Richardson. What they did not know was that as they passed through the Salt Creek Prairie in Young County, the same area where Britt Johnson had died four months before, they did so

Library of Congress
William T. Sherman

under the close watch of around a hundred Kiowas and allied warriors under the leadership of Kiowa chief Satanta, along with Big Bow, White Horse, Satank, and Big Tree. The watchful Indians did not know that the small military party included the most powerful general in the United States. Instead, they turned to their spiritual leader, Sky Walker the Owl Prophet, and asked if they should attack. Instead, he advised they wait for a more lucrative, and less well-defended, opportunity and claimed a vision of a plunder-laden load coming soon. The following day, a civilian wagon train, heavy with supplies bound for Fort Griffin, passed through the same valley. In a raid that would become known as the Warren Wagon Train Raid, the Indians attacked, torturing, killing, and mutilating many of the teamsters before escaping with most of the cargo and forty mules. The Indians then simply melted back to their reservation in Indian Territory.

One of the wounded teamsters managed to make his way to Fort Richardson that night and informed officials about the attack and its location. Shocked, Sherman ordered post commander Colonel Ranald Mackenzie and his troopers from the Fourth Cavalry to pursue the attackers, but they were not able to find the culprits. In the meantime, Sherman continued his trip northward to Fort Sill in Indian Territory—ironically paralleling the route the raiders took to the Kiowa reservation.

While drawing his government rations back on the Kiowa reservation, Satanta boasted openly about the successful raid, and word of this activity spread to officials at Fort Sill soon after Sherman's arrival. The general summoned the Indians to Col. Benjamin Grierson's headquarters at Fort Sill. There, on the porch, the two Union veterans confronted Kiowa chiefs Satanta, Satank, and Big Tree, and Sherman ordered a company of Buffalo Soldiers standing by to arrest them. He also directed that the three be sent back to Fort Richardson to stand trial for murder in a clear attempt to apply civil law to Indians. Satank tried to escape en route to Texas and his soldier escorts shot and killed him. A civilian jury in Jacksboro found Satanta and Big Tree guilty of murder and sentenced them to death, but Texas Governor E.J. Davis commuted their sentence to life in prison. Here both would serve as hostages to ensure good behavior from the rest of the Kiowas.

At the same time, the Warren Wagon Train Raid changed Sherman's approach to frontier defense. No longer satisfied that the Medicine Lodge Treaty had succeeded, the general now moved toward a much more aggressive stance in dealing with Indians in Texas. He ordered another show of force and directed Colonel Mackenzie to take the Fourth Cavalry and Tonkawa Scouts on the offensive into the Panhandle, to chastise Indians found there and convince them to accept their lot and return to the reservations.

Mackenzie's first two efforts met with mixed results. His first sweep, a six-week-long campaign starting in early August, encountered no Indians and his command returned to Forts Griffin and Richardson to resupply; by September 24 they were back at it. Starting on October 9, the troopers skirmished with Quahadi Comanches under Quanah Parker. That night, the Indians attacked Mackenzie's camp, turning the soldiers out of their beds and capturing nearly seventy government mounts. The next day, the Quahadis ambushed a column sent in pursuit, forcing the soldiers into a defensive perimeter until rescued by Mackenzie and his main force. On October 15, Mackenzie himself was lightly wounded as he tried to personally capture two isolated Quahadis in Blanco Canyon. After that, he broke contact and returned his men to their posts. While militarily inconclusive, the Army's raid into the Panhandle revealed that the Comanches maintained contact with Comancheros from New Mexico, continuing a trade in captives and guns that dated back to the Spanish Colonial era.

That winter and spring, Indians, settlers, and soldiers continued the frontier minuet of raiding, pursuit, and combat, with troops, pioneers, Kiowas, and Comanches dying in scores of private, intimate, gruesome battles. In April 1872 Kiowa leaders Big Bow and White Horse, along with Lone Wolf and his son Tau-ankia or Horseback, raided another government wagon train, this time at Howard's Wells, twenty-five miles southwest of present-day Ozona. After slaughtering seventeen Hispanic teamsters, the Kiowas, including this father and son team, fought off around fifty Buffalo Soldiers from the Ninth Cavalry, killing one soldier and mortally wounding a lieutenant. Horseback had also been wounded, and Lone Wolf nursed him back to the reservation where he recovered to fight again.

This constant skirmishing convinced U.S. leaders to unleash Mackenzie once again, and he resumed his campaign to force compliance with the Medicine Lodge Treaty. Starting on July 1, 1872, five companies of the Fourth Cavalry, aided by a company of the all-black Twenty-fourth Infantry and twenty Tonkawa scouts, moved northwest from Fort Richardson, again attempting to break the resistance of the non-cooperating renegades. On September 29, 1872, the soldiers discovered and attacked a major encampment of Quahadi and Kosoteka Comanches on McClellan Creek. In the brief but violent battle, both sides contended for the Indian horse herd, with the troopers seizing eight hundred ponies only to lose all but fifty that night. The Indians withdrew, leaving Mackenzie in possession of much of their camp supplies, as well as 130 women and children. Three soldiers lay dead and seven suffered wounds, but Federal bullets cut down nearly sixty Comanches. U.S. troops also recovered three Mexican captives. Mackenzie declared victory and returned to his base. Most of the Indians returned to their reservation, chastened.

During this brief thawing of relations between the government and the Indians of the South Plains, Kiowas hoped to gain the release of their most famous kinsmen, Satanta and Big Tree. Governor Davis agreed and released the two to the custody of the agent at Fort Sill. Even so, U.S. authorities warned, any mischief on their part, or that of any Kiowa, would land them back in prison.

Still, the raids continued. Horseback, back in full vigor after being wounded a year and a half earlier, accompanied several other young Kiowas—including his cousin, Guitain—and Comanches on a horse-stealing raid into Mexico, perhaps thinking that Mexicans were not off limits. On the return trip, Fourth Cavalry troops from Fort Clark patrolling north to Fort Concho surprised the Indians at Kickapoo Springs, just thirty miles southeast of their destination. Soldiers killed nine Indians, including Horseback and Guitan. When news reached the reservation, Lone Wolf was inconsolable.

In May 1874 the Kiowa war chief led an expedition to recover his son's bones. After arriving at Kickapoo Springs without trouble, he gingerly wrapped the remains of his son and his nephew in blankets and strapped them to his horse.

He then rode northwest, past Fort Concho, and conducted a night raid on a detachment of Ninth Cavalry troopers at Johnson Station on the Middle Concho River. Equipped with these soldiers' fresh, grain-fed mounts, Lone Wolf and his Kiowas avoided interception by pursuers from the Fourth Cavalry. At a rocky mount four miles north of present-day Loraine in Mitchell County, Lone Wolf buried the bones of his son and his nephew. He then swore revenge.

Despite this steady attrition on both sides, Indian raids continued on the frontier leading U.S. authorities to seek a permanent solution to the problem. As long as these malcontents could sustain themselves off of the reservation, they would continue to lead a double life, living peacefully on government support during the snows of winter only to take to the prairies when the weather warmed up. While Mackenzie had been trooping out from frontier Texas forts—crisscrossing the breaks along the Canadian River and the Caprock—to chase an elusive enemy, far to the north newcomers to the Kansas plains were getting rich. They, like the Comanches and Kiowa before them, were killing buffalo.

Hunting the Buffalo

What lured these men to Kansas was actually a nexus of Kansas plainsmen and New York City businessmen. Entrepreneurs in those two places had found a potential financial bonanza when a tannery in New York successfully processed Kansas buffalo hides for leather, creating an immediate and significant demand for the product. The pioneer of

J. Wright Mooar as portrayed at Frontier Texas

this effort, Vermont native J. Wright Mooar, had worked his way to the Kansas frontier by 1870. He labored for a while at Fort Hays, cutting wood for the fort and killing buffalo as a contract hunter. He then moved near Dodge City where railroad crews were busy in constructing tracks, and his heavy-barreled rifle provided meat to these hungry workers.

While in Dodge City, Mooar met Charles Myers and Charles Rath, two businessmen. Myers had gotten a contract from a London firm to supply them with one hundred buffalo hides so they could experiment in different techniques to tan the tough skins. He paid Mooar and Rath to go onto the Kansas plains to kill enough buffalo to fill the order. When they returned, they had more than enough. Mooar decided that he would take the excess hides and ship them to his brother John, a jewelry store clerk in New York City, to see if he could find a tanning firm there that might want them. John did so, and the tannery was so pleased with the quality that they immediately ordered two thousand more hides. News soon spread that a fortune could be made by anyone with a rifle and the will to use it on the giant herds of the Great Plains.

John Mooar left his jewelry-shop job in New York City to join his brother in Kansas in November 1872. The two joined into a partnership. Both hunted and freighted hides, and after each hunt they could return with as many as four thousand. Soon, hundreds of other men joined them, also seeking their fortunes.

As competition crowded the plains, the Mooar brothers decided that perhaps the buffalo hunting range should expand into the Texas Panhandle. They were concerned that the provisions of the Medicine Lodge Treaty prohibited white men from hunting there. J. Wright Mooar and another hunter, Steel Frazier, were elected by a delegation of hunters to travel to Fort Dodge to discuss the matter with its commander, Col. Richard I. Dodge. As commander of the troops in that post, Dodge was responsible for enforcement of the treaty and would be able to give them a definitive answer, they reasoned. They were elated, therefore, when Dodge's only advice was that they should "hunt buffalo where the buffalo are."

The Mooar brothers moved into the Texas Panhandle in July 1873 and established a hunting camp along the Canadian River. They were able to ship several thousand hides back to Dodge City, Kansas. When news of this achievement reached other hunters, the Mooars soon had plenty of company. Charles Rath even moved into the area and established a supply store and restaurant at the site of a long-abandoned trading post called Adobe Walls, twenty miles northeast of present-day Borger.

At last the government and free enterprise had created the conditions for the final reckoning with the Indians of the southern Great Plains. Whether it was a deliberate campaign against the logistics of the Indians, conceived by the great slash-and-burn strategists of the day, generals Sheridan and Sherman, or simply a happy coincidence, the days of the North American bison herd were numbered and with them the culture of the Plains Indians. With an estimated 1,500 hunting teams killing and skinning an average of fifty animals a day per team, there would come a day, and fairly soon, when buffalo would be an oddity on the prairies they had occupied for millennia. The Indians near the Fort Sill reservations knew that the time had come for a final stand.

Ranald S. Mackenzie and the Red River War

Indian mystics announced that the time for the final battle had arrived. Members of the Comanche, Kiowa, and Southern Cheyenne nations had become disgruntled with the U.S. government's failure to consistently hold up its end of the Medicine Lodge Treaty. Promised rations were often inedible, and white men from Kansas and Texas had now entered frequently onto reservation land to steal horses or hunt buffalo. Quaker Indian agents, who tried to protect their people from these white scoundrels, received no support from the military. Buffalo hunters from Kansas had already destroyed much of the northern bison herd, impoverishing the residents of the Cheyenne-Arapaho Reservation. With the dwindling herds, and with poor rations coming from the federal government, members of the Comanche, Kiowa, Cheyenne, and Arapaho tribes found themselves hungry and desperate. Before long they resorted to slaughtering their horses to feed their families.

In the late spring of 1874 Comanche medicine man Isatai called for a gathering to coincide with the Sun Dance—a Kiowa religious ceremony that had never been part of the Comanche tradition. Several hundred Comanches attended, including the young and charismatic war chief of the Quahadi band, Quanah Parker. The son of Peta Nacona and the former captive Cynthia Ann Parker, Quanah had risen to great power within the Quahadi band because of his strength and leadership. At the Sun Dance gathering, Isa-tai and Quanah began to recruit warriors to raid into Texas, promising supernatural help in their cause. Other veteran chiefs at the meeting, including Yamparika Comanches White Wolf and Sound-of-the-Sun, contemplated the expedition and pointed out that if Quanah intended to attack the real threat to their way of life, then he should kill the buffalo hunters. Soon leaders from the various tribes committed themselves and their followers to the fight, dabbing themselves with yellow paint that had been promised to turn away bullets. Impatient to start, the Comanches left behind most of the Kiowas, who were awaiting the climax of their religious ceremony.

In late June 1874 Quanah Parker led this massive war party of seven hundred Comanche, Kiowa, Cheyenne, and Arapaho warriors into the Texas Panhandle and on June 27 attacked a buffalo hunters' camp at Adobe Walls near the Canadian River. Even though they enjoyed overwhelming odds—there were only 28 hunters and merchants—the Indians could not close with the whites who, due to their trade, were armed with heavy bore, long-ranged rifles and plenty of ammunition and shot from behind strong defenses. After several days of fighting, Indians had killed only three hunters while losing dozens of their own to shots that were

Photograph by Lanney, 1868-1874. National Archives and Records Administration

Quanah Parker

once considered impossible. Even Quanah had been wounded by a ricochet, and his horse had been shot out from under him. When hunter Billy Dixon picked off a mounted warrior from a mile away, Quanah and his Indian coalition gave up the fight and withdrew on July 1. Their *puha*, it appeared, had failed. Behind them, lying still under the guns of the hunters, lay nearly seventy of their dead comrades and kinsmen.

The buffalo hunters also realized that something huge was afoot. They had witnessed the largest gathering of Indians of their day, and it became clear that the plains of Texas would be too hot for hunting. Most of the shooters and their teams of skinners returned to Kansas to await developments. Others flocked to nearby army posts, eager to sell their services as scouts and contractors. Quanah's warriors had succeeded in clearing the plains and had saved the herd for one more season, but a reckoning was coming.

In the meantime, the majority of the Kiowas had remained on the reservation waiting for the conclusion of their annual Sun Dance in early July, seeking divine guidance in determining their action. At the ceremony, most of the Kiowas agreed to return to the reservation agency with Chief Kicking Bird. About fifty, however, formed a war party at the insistence of Lone Wolf and the self-proclaimed Owl Prophet, Sky Walker. This group moved south into Texas, riding into Jack County.

They would collide with a squad of equally determined Texans. Just a few months before, the state of Texas had taken measures to augment U.S. forces in the region. Governor Richard Coke ordered the organization of the Frontier Battalion, six companies of the newly reconstituted Texas Rangers under the command of Major John B. Jones. From their camps stretching from the Rio Grande to the Red River, these semi-professional fighters would work against Indians, outlaws, and vigilantes in equal measure.

On July 12 this new force would get its initiation in Kiowa wrath when Lone Wolf and Sky Walker's warriors surprised them in the hotly contested Lost Valley near Jacksboro. After taking refuge in a draw, the Texans found themselves running short of ammunition and water. Two Rangers, David Bailey and Billy Glass, volunteered to make a dash for a nearby creek and fill canteens. Lone Wolf's men cut these troopers off from their comrades, killing Glass quickly. The Kiowas took Bailey alive. While the Rangers watched, Lone Wolf cut off portions of the man's body—fingers, ears, nose—slowly torturing him to death. At last he slit the man's throat, declaring his son, Horseback, to be avenged. The Indians withdrew, allowing the Rangers to recover their dead.

The turmoil of the summer of 1874 convinced the U.S. Army to whip the Comanches and Kiowas decisively. Gen. Sherman and his subordinate, Lt. Gen. Philip Sheridan, implemented a new strategy. They ordered that all Indians still on the reservation must register immediately at their agencies. Thus, any Indians coming back later could automatically be identified as returning war parties. Once the suspected war makers had been identified, they could be eliminated. Most of the Indians understood their tactics and moved to comply. As small groups returned they recognized that they needed to find a safe haven quickly. The reservations could no longer serve as their base.

Next, the U.S. Army would seek out the troublemakers, deny them sanctuary, and destroy their ability to live on the plains. The campaign would involve thousands of soldiers in five columns to descend on the Texas Panhandle from several directions, squeezing Quanah's warriors into their traditional hideouts in the canyons along the Caprock. There, the soldiers would move in and either destroy the Indians or force them to surrender.

The first column of this planned assault was a force of eight companies of the Sixth Cavalry and four companies of the Sixth Infantry from Fort Dodge, Kansas, under the command of Col. Nelson Miles. Col. Ranald Mackenzie brought a second column of eight companies of the Fourth Cavalry and five companies from the Tenth and Eleventh Infantry north from Fort Concho. Maj. William R. Price led a squadron of cavalry east from New Mexico, and Lt. Col. John W. Davidson and George P. Buell led their commands, including several troopers of Buffalo Soldiers from the Tenth Cavalry, west from Indian Territory.

In August U.S. Army soldiers moved onto the reservations to identify which Indians were peaceful and which were not.

Special Collections Branch, United States Army Military History Institute

Ranald S. Mackenzie in the mid-1870s

Most of the Arapahos submitted quickly, but most of the Cheyennes refused. Near Fort Sill, parts of Davidson's cavalry entered into a fight with some Comanche warriors, supported by Lone Wolf's recently returned Kiowas. Most of these Indians escaped to join the other warriors in Texas. In the end, the army listed five thousand Indians as hostile, twelve hundred of whom were warriors.

As August wore on, the sun-drenched plains of the Llano Estacado baked under a severe drought. In temperatures in excess of 110 degrees, Col. Miles marched his men south, and on August 30, near Palo Duro Canyon, they met a group of Cheyenne, Kiowa, and Comanche warriors. They succeeded only in driving the Indians onto the plains, but the soldiers could not press their pursuit because they had to find a source for water and supplies instead.

On September 7 the skies opened up in a torrential rainstorm, and Miles was able to meet up with Price's column coming from New Mexico. The temporary elation of these circumstances, however, quickly gave way to more difficulty for these men. Two days later, a band of Comanches and Kiowas attacked and besieged a supply train heading toward Miles. The Indians eventually abandoned the siege after three days, but the assault severely slowed Miles and Price in any advance.

Col. Ranald Mackenzie picked up the attack. He and his force had stockpiled supplies so they could move into the area unhindered by the perils of waiting for supply trains. They moved into the canyons of the Caprock in mid September. After thwarting a Comanche attempt to stampede his horses on September 27, Mackenzie ordered a swift attack on a Comanche camp in Palo Duro Canyon two days later. The assault proved devastating for the Indians. Waves of cavalry swept onto the canyon floor after a dangerous descent down the canyon walls. They laid waste to the camp, burning everything they could. Most importantly, they destroyed most of the Indian food supply and equipment and captured some 1,500 Indian horses. Mackenzie knew that mobility was the main asset of the Indian force, so he ordered a thousand of the ponies destroyed.

For the next three months, the army forces combed the Panhandle. The temperature dropped below freezing; cold, hungry, and demoralized, many of the Indians began to slowly move back to the reservations. Most of them, however, continued to resist for another few months. The weather and the constant presence of the U.S. troops in the area finally broke them. In February 1875 Lone Wolf and around five hundred Kiowas surrendered and returned to the reservation. A few weeks later eight hundred Cheyennes and their chief, Gray Beard, also surrendered. Then in June, Quanah Parker led his Quahadi band to Fort Sill, where they formally capitulated to Col. Mackenzie. Quanah's surrender marked the last of the organized resistance and ended the Red River War. For good measure, U.S. authorities hustled many of the more notorious Comanches and Kiowas to Fort Marion, Florida, to cool off for a few years.

Overall the military lessons of the Red River War were not lost on the leadership of the U.S. Army. The doctrine of total war, which Gen. Sherman had used so effectively in the Civil War against the Confederacy, was now once again successful on the frontier. From this point on, military strategy to subdue Indian tribes would include destroying the Indians' means of existence. Mackenzie had shown the willingness to do so at Palo Duro Canyon in killing a thousand Indian horses. But if the Indians could leave the reservation once, then they could do it again—unless their means of survival on the plains was taken away as well.

Like the angel with the flaming sword that blocked the return to Eden after the fall of man, the U.S. Army placed a permanent garrison on the eastern edge of the Texas

Panhandle denying the Indians access to this range forever. In June 1875 U.S. troops established Fort Elliot twenty-seven miles west of the Texas line, quartering more than two hundred men on a plateau overlooking Sweetwater Creek, beyond the North Fork of the Red River. Soldiers from here would patrol along the margins of the reservations, turning back any parties hoping once again to make a dash for freedom.

Chapter Six
Destruction of the Buffalo and the Rise of the Cattle Frontier, 1865-1880

In the winter of 1873–1874 Fort Worth resident J.B. Clack and a half-dozen companions made their way to Taylor County, Texas, to spend the winter hunting buffalo and to have a little "rough fun" on the frontier. They had not come to get rich, just merely to scout the land and see what lay beyond the horizon. They brought several ox-drawn wagons with them to carry any hides they might take, but for most of them it was a lark full of adventure, danger, and perhaps, potential.

Indians, of course, were a concern, but the men had agreed to look out for each other and to signal each other in case of a crisis. The first test of their warning system came soon after the group camped just north of Buffalo Gap. "One of the boys rambled off alone," wrote Mary Hampton Clack in her memoirs, *Early Days in West Texas*. She married J.B. two years after his buffalo hunt. "In a short time the camp was aroused by the firing of several shots in the direction he had gone. Not only that, but the shots were accompanied with yelling to better attract their attention." Grabbing their guns, the greenhorn hunters boiled out into the brush, hurrying to save their companion. "They were rather disappointed to find

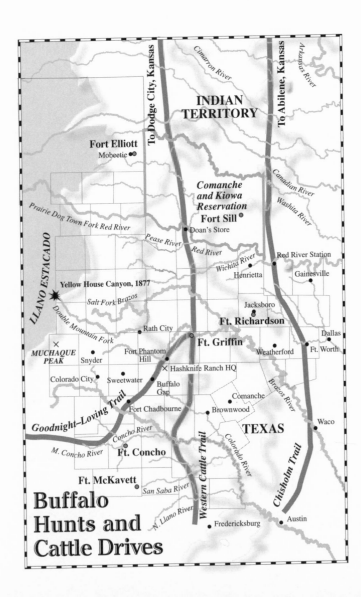

Buffalo
Hunts and
Cattle Drives

him hovering about the carcass of a huge buffalo he had killed. He had adopted this plan to secure help to convey the beast to camp."

These rookies got quite an education in the days that followed. For starters, they learned that buffalo hides are heavy. "The boys made what they considered a wonderful discovery," Clack continued, "namely that it was beyond the power of one man to lift a huge buffalo hide off the ground and place it on a wagon." They spent several hours trying different techniques, before "they were willing to give it up as an impossibility." They discovered that a diet of strictly buffalo left them craving other fare. Fortunately, the pecan trees along Elm Creek were loaded with turkeys. There were bears to hunt, too. It snowed more in Taylor County than in Tarrant County, and the group adapted its camp to best meet the weather. Then it warmed up as fast. The adventurers also noted the negative effects of using roasted prickly pears as a bread substitute after the designated cooks ate a pile then spent the next day vomiting or suffering from "the scours."

The friends also courted disaster. Unlike professional hunters, these men used any ersatz technique they could dream of to close in on buffalo. One tracked a sizable herd to a mesquite flat near Elm Creek, probably within the present-day city limits of Abilene. In order to get a closer shot, the hunter slipped down into a side draw of the creek to continue his approach under cover. While deep in the ravine, "his attention was arrested by a rumbling noise closely allied to thunder," Clack wrote. The man hesitated, then saw scores of panicked buffalo heading down into the head of the draw and rumbling straight for him. "He glanced about for some means of escape, but there was none that he could see." Instead, he backed into the high bank, and hoped for the best. When the leader came opposite him, the hunter prodded him with his gun barrel in an attempt to change his course. "Shocked, surprised, the buffalo swerved toward the opposite side of the draw and hurried on a little faster," Clack remembered. "The rest took the 'cue,' each going through the same swerving motion. This then was one of the narrow escapes from what might so easily have ended in a tragedy."

Eventually, the Indians came as well. Early one morning, before the camp had really started stirring, one of the men slipped off into the brush for some privacy but came running back shouting that Indians were at hand. This shocked the rest awake, and they rolled out of their blankets, according to Clack, "just in time to get a look at the band of about one dozen painted and feather-decorated Redskins hurrying past." Fortunately for these tenderfoots, the raiders were in a hurry. "Although close enough to have conversed with the buffalo hunters, yet the Indians did not pause to engage them in controversy nor even glance their way." Apparently these marauders, most likely Comanches, did not consider this bunch of white men much of a threat. "However," added the writer, "they stopped long enough to cut the rope, and take possession of a saddle pony." J.B. Clack had staked his horse only a short distance from camp, but now he watched as the animal and its new owner loped north across the prairie.

Courtesy of Judge Steve M. King, Fort Worth,Texas

Group of Texan Hunters

"Soon after this rather significant episode the hunters broke camps and started for home."

What Clack and his companions had witnessed was a raiding party returning from several weeks of mischief in Brown County. Although obviously spooked by the incident, this band of explorers, for all of their inexperience, had seen the potential of this new country. Even as U.S. Army soldiers actively campaigned against the Indians later in 1874, buffalo hunters—both professional and amateur—rushed into the vacuum left on the plains by the suppression of its native inhabitants.

The Buffalo Slaughter in Texas

With the northern Panhandle clearly still dangerous and the scene of most of the fighting, shooters followed the lead of men like Clack and his companions and worked the southern herd from the east and south in the winter of 1874-1875. There had already been forays made onto the plains from places like Brownwood and Comanche. Others headed up from Saint Angela near Fort Concho. Mostly these were small, tenuous operations and did not come close to the large commercial enterprises of the Kansas plains. Some left after a season of sport, but other newcomers—like the team of John W. Poe, Joe McCombs, and John C. Jacobs—headed out of Fort Griffin to try their luck.

Poe had become a buffalo hunter not by design but because it was a way to experience the excitement of the frontier. "It's just what I've been wanting to do all my life," Poe told a companion. "Ever since I was a little shaver, and my grandfather read the *Leatherstocking Tales* to me, I've wanted to live on the frontier—be a part of it. I'm not worried about dangers—Indians or whatever else may be out there." He had left his native Kentucky, done various jobs including railroad construction, and had wound up in Kansas City. There, he had learned of the money to be had in hunting and used his savings to buy a horse and supplies to get him to

Fort Griffin. Once there, he scrounged about for ways to make enough money to start an outfit of hunters. He met another Kentuckian—Jacobs—and the two became partners.

The route to buffalo hunting glory was winding. First the two tried their hand at the very thing they had left Kentucky to avoid: farming. "Both were young, strong, energetic and—very important on a pioneer homestead—ingenious," wrote Sophie Poe, whom John married several years after arriving in Texas. "They became masters of make shift." Before long, the industrious plowmen had a fine stand of corn. As the plants began to tassel and the pair began to envision the money they would make from the crop, grasshoppers arrived and destroyed the field. Busted, the two turned to wolfing—hunting wolves for their pelts. After six months they sold $489 worth of lobo skins. That winter, the duo used their wolfing money to buy a wagon and supplies and received a contract to cut wood for the garrison of Fort Griffin, earning a dollar a cord for 1,600 cords. Moving into the timber north of present-day Clyde, the two managed three cords a day each. The contract took eight months to fulfill.

After nearly two years of hard labor and disappointments since arriving in Northwest Texas, the Kentuckians moved to a more lucrative profession. "Their return to Fort Griffin created something of a sensation," Sophie wrote in her memoir, *Buckboard Days*. On their way to deliver their last load of wood, they ran across an old associate, Joe McCombs. "Hellow, you God-Forsaken Heathens," the man called out, "come back to civilization did you? Well I was thinking the other day that, if you didn't come back soon, you'd turn into a couple of them damn Comanches." After a reunion with this old acquaintance, Poe and Jacobs enjoyed the relative comforts of the town. The word on every corner, though, seemed to be about hunting on the plains. "Very naturally, the two successful woodcutters caught 'buffalo fever' and, after a few days of loafing about Fort Griffin," Sophie remembered, "they decided to have a fling at the game."

They put their woodcutting income to work. They spent half on supplies for several months in the field. They also invited McCombs to join them as a skinner. The most important purchase, though, was two Sharps "Big-Fifty" rifles. Drifting out to the vicinity of Paint Creek in present-day Jones County, the two went to work. After several months and two separate hunts, the three-man team hauled back two thousand hides. Their luck, it would appear, had changed.

Before long, professional and seasoned Kansas hunters began turning up on the Texas frontier, too. Hidemen Jim White and Mike O'Brien came down from Dodge City to the Clear Fork country. They reported that the Northwest Texas frontier looked promising but added that five hundred miles lay between the heart of the Texas buffalo range and the nearest shipping point at Denison. They gave Fort Griffin high marks, though, for location as a base for entering the plains.

After the defeat of the Comanches and Kiowas, the destruction of the southern herd would be systematic and efficient. A building crescendo of hunting outfits jostled and scrambled to establish the best base for the hunt, and clever businessmen were happy to assist. Hunters returned from the north, moving out of Dodge City within weeks of Quanah Parker's surrender in the early summer of 1875. Charles Rath, with the assistance of Robert M. Wright, the post sutler of Fort Dodge, also returned and established a store and supply settlement in the shadow of Fort Elliot. Originally called Hidetown, then Sweetwater, it soon blossomed into the town of Mobeetie. From there, hunters prowled the grasslands, killing an astounding number of animals and stripping them of their hides before heading back to base. Buyers also came, bidding on the best specimens before bundling them into bales and consigning them to shippers hauling them on to Dodge City.

These new men were scientific. Using excellent rifles and superior techniques, they were soon knocking down scores of animals a day. Shooters began to experiment with different firearms, and the weapons industry back east kept pace. "The man I sold my old .44 to killed 119 buffalo in one day with it," wrote Kansas hunter R.W. Snyder. "That beats me with my Big .50—as 93 is the most that I ever killed in one day."

The outfits all followed a similar makeup. A typical hunting team consisted of around four men and included at least one shooter accompanied by skinners and perhaps a camp manager and teamster. As the prime killing season ran during the winter months on the Texas range, coinciding with migration patterns and hide quality, these parties had to pack and plan for three months of potentially brutal conditions on the prairie. To maximize profits, a shooter might pack out a hundred rounds of large caliber ammunition a day, requiring the group to carry some 250 pounds of lead, more than 4,000 primers, and up to 100 pounds of gunpowder for reloading cartridges.

The work was tough. During a typical day, this band of plainsmen would scout the area for a herd, pick out a small clump of animals, and approach them downwind as close as possible. Once within reliable range, the hunter would then set up a "stand" or firing position, and, using crossed sticks or a tripod to brace his gun, begin the work. "If a herd was lying at rest," wrote hunter W. Skelton Glenn, a shooter "would pick out some buffalo that was standing up on watch and shoot his ball in his side so that it would not go through. A buffalo shot in this manner would merely hump up his back as if he had the colic and commence to mill around." By mortally wounding the animal but not killing it outright, the hunter avoided spooking the herd. "This was termed mesmerizing the buffalo," Glenn explained, "which proved to be the most successful way of killing buffalo." As this animal stumbled about, the other animals would not be concerned, allowing them to be taken systematically while they rested. Once this small bunch had played out, the shooter took up another stand and began the process again.

Skinners earned their pay. After the last carcass of a group of buffalo hit the ground, the rest of the team went to work. Driving a wagon into the midst of the dead and dying, the skinners would began taking the hides, using their wagon and mules to peel the animals and roll the heavy bodies over. These men did heavy work and were covered in the gore asso-

Archives and Information Services Division, Texas State Library and Archives Commission

Hunters skinning buffalo

ciated with processing large game. The speed in which they did their chore usually dictated how many animals could be taken in a day. "The best skinners were artists at their work," wrote Poe. "The best skinner . . . prided himself on being able to skin from fifty to sixty buffalo a day, without regarding it as an extra heavy day's job." As the season progressed, the plains of West Texas became dotted with the rotting carcasses of buffalo, stripped of their hides but their meat and bones left for scavengers.

These newcomers could make a pretty good living by killing buffalo. Each hide would fetch between $1.50 and $3, but only one in three was considered to be of market quality. Even so, the sale of just 140 hides would equate the average annual income of the Texan of that time period. Skinners made less than hunters, but both ended up with a decent income. Buyers would come to well-known rendezvous places like Buffalo Gap, Fort Phantom Hill, Fort Griffin, or Mobeetie to buy the hides, then consign them to freighters to get them to shipping points. This activity nurtured other industries. Hotels and restaurants sprang up to house and feed transient populations. Stores sold them guns and ammunition, and freighters made money by the mile.

An estimated 1,500 hunters came to Texas. With each team taking between 50 and 100 hides a day for three months a year, the great southern herd would soon dwindle to oblivion. Some citizens of Texas began to fear the loss of something precious if hunters drove the buffalo to extinction. In 1875 a bill came before the Texas Legislature to protect the buffalo from such wanton destruction.

Gen. Phil Sheridan, commander of the U.S. Army's Department of the Southwest and frustrated by years of fighting the Indians of the South Plains, was furious. In a fit of pique, he suggested that buffalo hunters had "done more in the last two years . . . to settle the vexed Indian question than the entire regular army has done in the last 30 years." If left alone, he argued, they would end the long history of Indian depredations forever. "They are destroying the Indian's commissary," he wrote. "It is a well-known fact that an army losing its base of supplies is placed at a great disadvantage." The veteran Civil War campaigner simply applied some of the lessons he had learned.

Sheridan argued that the hunters should be encouraged by the State of Texas. "Send them powder and lead, if you will, and for the sake of lasting peace, let them kill, skin, and sell until they have exterminated the buffalo." Once the animals were gone, he believed, Texas would enjoy an economic boom. "Your prairies would be covered with speckled cattle and the festive cowboy, who follows the hunter as the second forerunner of civilization."

In full sympathy with these views, professional hunters aggressively flanked the southern herd from the east. The settlement known as The Flats, below Government Hill at Fort Griffin, boomed. "It was in the fall of '76, I was engaged in the back end of a storehouse and heard someone ask the boys who ran the shebang," remembered Fort Griffin merchant Frank Conrad. "I went forward and met the man. He wanted some ammunition, and asked if I had plenty. I told him I had." The hunter placed an order for three kegs of powder and about four hundred pounds of lead. "It nearly took my breath away," Conrad said. "I asked him if he was shooting artillery and what his occupation was. He said he was a buffalo hunter. I told him that I had only two-thirds a keg, and as a general thing only sold a keg in three months."

This shaggy haired man was the harbinger of things to come. "I had a lot of talk with the man and found he was the fore-runner of a lot of Kansas men coming to Texas to kill buffalo," Conrad continued. "After thinking the matter over I decided to send to Bridgeport, Connecticut, after twenty-five kegs, and before it came there were men who arrived that would have taken twice as much."

From the fall of 1874 to the spring of 1879, this one-time "scab town" on the margins of a military post became the principal base for hunters moving west onto the buffalo range. Conrad, a Confederate veteran and experienced merchant who had served as the post trader of Forts McKavett and Griffin, became one of the greatest beneficiaries as stores like his fueled the hunting industry. The men who started it all, J. Wright and John Wesley Mooar, along with a freighter they had teamed up with named Pete Snyder, moved their base to Fort Griffin as well. Soon, Kansas hide firms opened branch offices. As one resident, John Chadbourne Irwin, remembered, "There was buffalo hunters, hide money, trail herd money and soldier money." Despite the boom, a reporter for a Fort Worth newspaper described the settlement as "nothing save a few dobie and picket houses, corrals, and immense stacks of buffalo hides."

After more than a year of steady killing, hunters had to travel farther into the range to find profitable herds. Merchants like Rath were eager to keep up. He entered into a new partnership, this time with William McDole Lee and his associate Albert Reynolds. Lee, who ran the official store for Fort Elliot, headed an empire of his own, making money off of the military, Indian reservations, or buffalo hunters since his partnership with Reynolds seven years before. He even

Buffalo hunters campsite

claimed hide outlets in New York and Chicago. With his solid financial backing, Rath led an ox-drawn caravan due south of Mobeetie, moving some 150 miles until coming nearly even with a azimuth shot 60 miles west from Fort Griffin. In December 1876 Rath established his second trading outlet, Rath City, the Dodge City trader competing directly with established frontier Texas firms. By early the next year two saloons, a dance hall, a restaurant, and a Chinese laundry stood near his store, a transient population of around five hundred camped nearby, and wagonloads of hides moved north to market.

The Hunters' War

That would prove to be a momentous winter. At almost the precise moment that Rath had hammered his tent stakes into the ground and unloaded wagons within sight of the Double Mountains, Indians under the Quahadi Comanche Chief Black Horse made one last attempt to regain their freedom. Leaving the reservation in a heavy snow, more than 170 men, women, and children evaded U.S. troops trying to track them and headed for the canyons of the Caprock.

After making camp, the warriors began hunting the buffalo hunters. On February 1, 1877, they crept up on Marshall Sewell, waited patiently until he fired the last of his ammunition at some buffalo, then closed in for the kill. They raided several hunting outfits as well, plundering their camps. A general alarm swept the plains. A party of around forty hunters from Rath City headed up the Salt Fork of the Brazos, found and buried Sewell's mutilated body, and then tracked the culprits, skirmishing with the Indians before returning with one man, a mixed-race hunter named Spotted Jack, mortally wounded. By the end of February almost every hunting party had come in from the range and clustered near settlements for protection.

The residents of Rath City refused to let these Indians win. The hunters held a meeting to gauge popular sentiment for a campaign to rid the plains of the marauders. After an acrimonious debate, several dozen veteran plainsmen organized an expedition, leaving Rath City on March 4 and following the Double Mountain Fork of the Brazos toward the

Caprock. After two weeks of searching, the hunters located Black Horse and his band at Yellow House Canyon in present-day Lubbock. After a gun battle of several hours, the hunters retreated with three men wounded, one mortally. By March 27 the hunters returned to Rath City, tired and chastened.

The Indians continued their dash for freedom forcing the U.S. Army to respond as well. Soldiers of Company G, Tenth Cavalry under Capt. Philip L. Lee left Fort Griffin, climbed the Caprock and attacked the Indian camp on May 4, 1877, near Silver Lake in present-day Cochran County. The troopers killed four Comanches and captured six women and sixty-nine horses, but lost their company sergeant in the battle. Although punished, the Indians remained out of the reach of the army and headed deeper onto the Llano Estacado.

Their harassment of buffalo hunters would continue. Later in the month, some of Black Horse's Quahadis raided Rath City, stealing more than a hundred horses. On another occasion, several young Comanches rode brazenly down the main street, daring the hunters to follow. Jim Harvey and twenty-four hidemen he gathered into a company—and calling themselves the "forlorn hope"—took the bait. Two months later, on July 10, Company A, Tenth Cavalry left Fort Concho to hunt for the Indians as well, and on July 17 the two parties met near Muchaque Peak in Bordon County. The combined force of nearly seventy men pushed deep into the Llano Estacado, but found themselves lost and short of water. The hunters, chafing under Captain Nicholas Nolan's leadership, abandoned the soldiers and made their way to safety.

The troopers were not so lucky. Without guides or water, the unit fell apart. Men deserted, heading back the way they had come, desperate for water. Eventually thirty-six of the forty-man company returned, leaving four of their own dead of thirst on the Llano Estacado.

Black Horse and his people were also suffering that summer. With the thrill of the spring turning into the dry monotony of summer, and with the looming threat of military action against them, the Indians began to have second thoughts. The buffalo, too, were becoming scarce, proving the case General Sheridan had presented to the people of Texas. By fall, Black Horse and the remaining Quahadis called it quits and trickled voluntarily back to the reservations to accept their punishment.

At the height of this excitement, Rath and Conrad joined forces to create one of the most successful hide-related commercial enterprises on the South Plains. Already in two different enterprises with two different partners, Rath aimed to continue riding the boom and, ever the entrepreneur, headed east to Fort Griffin. There, with his new partner, his store began posting days where the income exceeded $4,000, most of it from the sales of guns and ammunition. More lead left that town in a month than was sold in many settled states in a year.

The fortunes could not last forever. The peak killing season was the winter of 1876-1877. During this easy era, J. Wright Mooar added 8,200 hides to a career that would eventually account for an estimated 20,000 buffalo. Joe McCombs' outfit killed 7,200 in the same time span; the team of Poe and Jacobs killed around 12,000 in their four-year partnership. The 1877-1878 season started well, but by March 1878 yields were a third of what they had been. The age of the buffalo hunter was passing. By October of that year, journalists in the *Fort Griffin Echo* crowed that the next boom had arrived, and that "trail traffic is replacing the buffalo trade."

Merchants and hunters alike, spoiled by the days of easy money, turned to other lines of work. Charlie Rath and Frank Conrad parted company in 1879. Meteoric Rath City lay abandoned. The Mooar brothers, needing cash, contracted to salvage what could be had from the remains of the town, packed it into wagons, and hauled it back north from whence it came. Their freighter companion, Pete Snyder, who had opened a trading post in the waning days of the hunt, saw a new settlement springing up around his place on Deep Creek, taking its name from his store. Within months, all of these men and many like them, who had been so instrumental in the buffalo slaughter, turned to other fields. Many followed the examples of their neighbors and—proving Gen. Sheridan a prophet—raised cattle.

The Cow Men

Hunting buffalo held little appeal for John Simpson, who instead followed a more traditional route to wealth when he moved his Hashknife Ranch to northern Taylor County in 1875. Recently cleared of the native beasts by the rough and tumble hunters whose shots he could still hear in the distance, the location north of Buffalo Gap was a desolate one—perfect for running open-range cattle—and now devoid of grazing competitors. He located his first headquarters in a dugout in the bank of Cedar Creek, and from there Simpson oversaw a growing operation, branding several thousand calves every spring. The ranch employed several cowboys to watch the margins of this growing herd in this sprawling, unfenced, sea of grass, and their lives could sometimes be dangerous.

Even with the threat of Indian raids receding fast, these young hands learned that frontier Texas still held plenty of hazards. In the late 1870s one of Simpson's teenaged cowboys fell from his horse, sustaining mortal internal injuries. His dying plea to his fellow cowboys was not to be buried in such a desolate place, but for his body to be taken back to Weatherford and to lie in a grave next to his mother. With cattle to watch and work to be done, however, his friends could not heed his dying wish, and they buried him on the lonely prairie. Today, there are at least three gravesites north of present-day Abilene that purport to belong to this cowboy, but the exact location of his nameless grave will never be known.

The tale of this dying wish was told for years before an anonymous author submitted the saga as a poem entitled "Dying Cowboy" to a folklore publication in 1910. Eventually, this eulogy was put to a tune that would become one of the most popular songs of early western music—"Bury Me Not on the Lone Prairie"—twenty-nine verses in its most lengthy version. By the 1930s even President Franklin Roosevelt claimed the song as his favorite.

The themes that resonate from this poem illustrate the continuing difficulties of life on the Texas frontier after the Civil War. As soon as the Confederacy came to an end, the Texas frontier appeared to be a true land of opportunity to many, and they came seeking a new start in conquering the frontier. Some hunted buffalo, many punched cattle. But for a few, like the young cowboy on the Hashknife Ranch, this frontier borderland could still exact a price.

Making of the Cattle Kingdom

The Civil War had a tremendous impact on the future development of the former Confederate states. The South lay in tatters from four years of destruction and deprivation. The labor system of slavery, held on to at such a great cost, had given way to a new social structure fraught with problems. But in the midst of this chaos, one former Confederate state forged a new course. That state was Texas.

Livestock would truly set Texas apart after the Civil War. All of the former Confederate states had been major livestock producers before the war. In fact, livestock had represented the most valuable agricultural commodity in most southern states in the antebellum period. But the devastation of herds during the war, combined with the astronomical prices for cotton at the end of the conflict, convinced most Southerners to turn over their futures to the white fiber. They planted cotton. State after state revised their open-range laws and implemented fence requirements for livestock. Texas, however, was the only state where the war resulted in a substantial increase in livestock production.

Texas drew thousands of southern immigrants after the Confederacy fell, and many of them went into livestock raising. Enough cattle had roamed freely and multiplied on the prairies of West Texas during the war that energetic young men and their families could come to Texas, set up a small homestead, and round up a herd quickly. Contemporary publications even stated that entrepreneurial cattlemen could start with nothing and become completely independent financially within two years.

The main difficulty Texans encountered at the end of the war was in finding markets. They could raise cattle quite cheaply, but to make a profit they needed buyers. It became known that northern buyers paid up to ten times the amount Texans received for their stock at southern ports. This news induced Texans to drive their cattle overland for hundreds of miles to reach the northern markets. Trail drives made possible the great post-war cattle kingdom. Between 1866 and 1880 more than 4.2 million head of cattle were driven to markets in Kansas and Missouri, and to stock northern ranges. Texans took great pride in their successful cattle endeavors, and local newspapers constantly reported the status of each year's cattle drives. In June 1870 the *Galveston Daily News* announced that, "ninety thousand head of beeves and thirty thousand head of stock cattle have left Texas, and are now on the road to Abilene

[Kansas]. With the arrivals already reported, this makes one hundred and fifty thousand head of cattle to be sold in that market the present season. It has been predicted that the number would reach two hundred thousand." Perhaps the most staggering statistic—the figure that sets Texas agriculture apart from the rest of the Lower South by 1880—is that livestock in Texas was worth sixty-nine percent of the total agricultural worth of the state (a significant difference from the thirty-eight percent livestock represented for the rest of the Lower South).

Goodnight-Loving Trail

George Reynolds was typical of this southern stock-raising mindset. An Alabamian by birth, he had come to Texas as a toddler in 1847. His family farmed and raised cattle there before pushing on to the Palo Pinto County town of Golconda in 1859. Young Reynolds, now fifteen, carried the mail on horseback thirty-five miles between this frontier outpost and Weatherford, the last bastion of civilization at the time. During the Civil War, he served with Company E, Nineteenth Texas Cavalry under Brigadier General William Henry Parsons, campaigning in Louisiana and Arkansas before returning home wounded late in the war. Already a seasoned man at age twenty-three, Reynolds set out on yet another adventure in October 1865, when he and two companions drove a small herd of beeves from Palo Pinto County to New Mexico following the old Butterfield Stage route to the Pecos, then up that stream to Fort Sumner.

Reynolds blazed a trail that would make many men wealthy, and he set the tone for a new industry that would epitomize the Texas Frontier. The next year, he moved with his family onto the excellent range near the Clear Fork of the Brazos, just five miles from the ruins of Camp Cooper, and began gathering his cattle for another drive. That same year, 1866, two other of the most energetic cattlemen of the Texas frontier—Charles Goodnight and Oliver Loving—were playing a significant role in the settlement of the region, and their participation in the post-war cattle industry made them legendary in the story of the borderland.

Oliver Loving was born in Kentucky in 1812. In the 1840s he moved with his family to Texas, and by the late 1850s he had settled in what would become Palo Pinto County. He had a thousand-acre ranch and regularly drove his cattle to various markets. When his nineteen-year-old son drove his herd to Illinois on the Shawnee Trail, gaining a significant profit, Loving learned that long-distance drives could be quite remunerative. He organized two other drives before the Civil War—one to Illinois and one to Colorado—with the help of a young newcomer to the county, Charles Goodnight. Both trips brought great success. During the Civil War, the Confederate government commissioned Loving to drive cattle to the Mississippi River to supply Confederate troops. He did so, but when the war ended, the defunct Rebel government owed him an uncollectible $250,000. At the end of the war, Loving was near bankruptcy, but he still had access to large numbers of Texas cattle, and he knew that somewhere

George Reynolds as portrayed at Frontier Texas

there was a market willing to pay handsomely for them. It was at this point that he renewed his partnership with Charles Goodnight.

Goodnight was born in Illinois in 1836, and at age eleven he accompanied his family to Milam County, Texas. He learned to ride and shoot as a youngster, and he managed the family plantation for a few years. In the mid 1850s Goodnight formed a partnership with his step-brother, John Wesley Sheek, and the two began a cattle ranch on the Brazos River in Milam County. In 1857 the two men relocated their herd to the Keechi Valley in Palo Pinto County. Goodnight supplemented the ranch income by driving freight to Houston and back, but when Sheek got married, Goodnight took over supervision of the cattle operation. Goodnight also gave his services as a scout to Capt. J.J. Cureton's rangers, and in this capacity he discovered the trail to Comanche Chief Peta Nacona's camp on the Pease River in 1860. He informed Cureton and Capt. Lawrence "Sul" Ross of the location, leading to their attack on the camp, and the subsequent recapture of Cynthia Ann Parker. He spent most of the Civil War in efforts to chase Indians on the frontier, and in 1864 he returned to Palo Pinto County to try to rebuild his cattle business. At the end of the war, he had begun a new herd in Throckmorton County near Elm Creek. In September 1865 Comanches ran off nearly two thousand head of his cattle. He, too, was now ready to find a distant market where beef prices were high so he could rebuild his business with the profits.

The fifty-five-year-old Loving and his thirty-one-year-old protégé Goodnight hatched a plan that would make both of their fortunes. Perhaps based on Reynolds's experience, they learned that army posts in New Mexico would pay top dollar for beef, so the two combined their herds and in the spring of 1866 organized a drive leaving from Fort Belknap. Like Reynolds, they drove southwest to the Pecos River, following the old Butterfield Overland Mail route, then crossed at Horsehead Crossing and on to Fort Sumner, New Mexico. This drive, though, was much larger than Reynolds's and numbered eighteen cowhands driving hundreds of beef and stocker cattle. Perhaps the most trusted in the outfit was Bose Ikard, a newly freed slave from Parker County, of whom Goodnight would later say: "He was my detective, banker, and everything else . . . I trusted him more than any living man." Also on this drive, the partners used the first chuck wagon—a mobile commissary—for feeding the hands.

The drive arrived at Fort Sumter and brought a handsome profit for the partners. In the process, the two had created the Goodnight-Loving Trail—one of the most heavily used cattle trails of the frontier. After receiving $12,000 in gold from the army for this shipment of beef, Goodnight returned to Weatherford to start a second herd while Loving continued on with the stock cattle to Denver. The two reunited in New Mexico and started a ranch forty miles from Fort Sumner with the cattle Goodnight brought in; they were soon making a steady living.

The demand for Texas beef only increased as more troops moved west, and Indians moved to reservations where they would be fed by the U.S. government. To keep up, the two returned to Texas in the Spring of 1867, and started a third bunch of cattle on the trail. Heavy rains and Indian threats slowed this drive significantly, so Loving determined to move ahead of the herd to start the bidding process. Loving took one hand, Bill Wilson, with him, and he promised Goodnight that they would travel only at night through areas known to contain hostile Indians.

After two nights' travel, Loving became impatient and the pair set out during the day. At two in the afternoon, Wilson spotted several hundred Comanches closing on them from the southwest. The two men rode hard for the only cover around—the Pecos River about four miles away. Outpacing their pursuers, the men reached the hundred-foot bluff overlooking the river, scrambled down the incline, dismounted, and hitched their horses. They crossed the river and found a fortunate hiding place against the bank wall in the midst of a canebrake. The location also had a ledged cliff to protect them overhead, and a sand dune on the river side that guarded them from shots fired from the opposite side of the waterway.

The Indians soon had the two horses, and turned their attentions to the beasts' owners. The warriors quickly discovered the fire power the two cowmen had available when Loving used his Henry Rifle to shoot the first Indian to approach the dune. The Indians laid back, shooting into the stronghold. After several hours of this siege, one of the

Comanches called out in Spanish for the men to come out for a council. Realizing that their situation was probably hopeless, the two men decided to risk climbing onto the dune to discuss the situation with their attackers. Wilson stood to talk as Loving rose behind him, his rifle at the ready. As soon as they emerged, however, a Comanche shot crashed into Loving's wrist and entered his side. The cowmen scrambled quickly back into cover.

Wilson tended Loving's wounds as the Indians shot high-arching arrows into the redoubt throughout the night. Loving finally begged Wilson to escape under cover of darkness to report the attack to Goodnight and to tell his family of his fate. Wilson reluctantly agreed and left Loving with five pistols and a rifle. He pulled off his boots and clothes, quietly slipped into the river, and swam away unnoticed by the Indians. Wilson walked dozens of miles barefoot on the hot, torturous terrain, wearing only his underwear, but he reached Goodnight.

The herdsmen set out immediately with a rescue party, arriving at the site of the attack three days after the siege began. With no Indians in sight, Goodnight found the blood-soaked hole where Loving had lain. Attached to a bush nearby Goodnight found an Indian drawing on one of Loving's journal pages, but no other indication of his partner's fate. Goodnight assumed that Loving had perished and had been swept away by the river current.

He was wrong. After fending off further attacks for two days and nights, Loving decided that Wilson had not made it back to the herd. When he had not heard any sounds of Indians for several hours, he correctly assumed that the Comanches had given up on him, so he made his way to the river. He swam and crawled upriver for several miles, then collapsed near death under a tree. A group of Mexican traders found him there and carried him on their wagon to Fort Sumner. His wounds, however, had become infected, and Loving died of gangrene on September 25, 1867.

Before Loving died, Goodnight reached the fort to sit by his partner's side. Loving made a death-bed plea to be buried in Texas. Goodnight assured him that it would be so. Although Goodnight had Loving buried in a temporary grave at Fort Sumner while he drove the cattle farther north to Colorado, he later had the body exhumed and carried home. Despite this tragedy, their names lived on in the Goodnight-Loving Trail and their efforts helped to bring the cattle indus-try to full flower on the Texas frontier.

Ironically, George Reynolds would be seriously wounded within months of Loving's mortal injury. That April, while serving with a posse trailing Indian horse thieves as they escaped from the Clear Fork country, Reynolds took an arrow in the abdomen that, from all appearances, should prove fatal. Carried home by his brothers, everyone in his family began the death vigil. Amazingly, he recovered, but with the steel arrowhead still in him. He married Bettie Matthews, daughter of a ranching neighbor, three months later and gained an additional two hundred head of cattle to add to the eight hundred he already owned. The next year, in perfect health, he trailed this herd all the way to California, realizing a staggering profit. He would continue to drive cattle for more than two decades. In 1883, while on business in Kansas City, a surgeon removed the bothersome point after it had worked its way to just under the skin of his back. Reynolds had the steel arrow head made into a watch fob, and carried it with him throughout the rest of his career, amassing an empire of nearly 500,000 acres of ranch land and a fortune to go with it.

Chisholm Trail

Although markets in New Mexico and Colorado had lured Reynolds, Goodnight, and Loving, the vast majority of cattlemen on the Texas frontier turned their eyes northward in search of profits. Problems from the past, however, stood in the way of successful drives north. Both Missouri and Kansas had passed laws banning Texas herds from crossing their borders because of Texas Fever carried on tick-bearing Longhorns. Despite this quarantine, the demand for Texas beef in the East was increasing, creating a growing demand for drives to resume.

In the spring of 1867, Illinois businessman Joseph G. McCoy found a means to supply his home state with Texas cattle. He convinced the Kansas Pacific Railroad to lay a spur track to the small village of Abilene, Kansas, just on the edge of the quarantine area. He moved his operation to the hamlet and built cattle pens and loading facilities in preparation to receive large numbers of Texas cattle. He then sent word to Texas that Abilene was now ready to receive their herds. The first year McCoy shipped on the railroad 35,000 head out of his Abilene facility back East. Each year afterward, the number doubled until 1871, when he shipped an astounding 600,000 head of Texas cattle.

To get there, Texas drovers pushed their cattle along a route that would become known as the Chisholm Trail. Unlike the Goodnight-Loving Trail, this path was not named for the first cattlemen to travel it. The first herd on the route belonged to O.W. Wheeler and his partners. They had purchased 2,400 steers in San Antonio in 1867 with the intention of driving them to California through Indian Territory. When they reached the Canadian River, however, instead of turning west they decided to follow wagon tracks headed north. These tracks, which eventually took them to Abilene, Kansas, were those created by a Cherokee-Scot freight hauler named Jesse Chisholm. He had begun his trade route from his home near modern Wichita, Kansas, to many of the Indian camps in the Indian Territory.

What evolved was known as the Chisholm Trail. For its first few hundred miles, the drivers actually followed the old Shawnee Trail from San Antonio through Austin to Waco. From there the new route split off and headed through Fort Worth, passing east of Decatur, and on into Indian Territory at Red River Station. Once in Indian Territory it headed north to Abilene. As Texas cattlemen drove ever larger herds to their Kansas destination, they tended to push the animals about ten or twelve miles a day. The herds generally spread out in between rivers to graze along the route and were only gathered close at crossings. In good conditions, the rangy Longhorn steers could even gain weight on the trip. The typical drive included a trail boss, ten to twelve cowboys, a horse wrangler, and a cook.

One difficulty that began to emerge with the Chisholm Trail was that it moved through areas that were becoming more populated after the Civil War. As farmers built homesteads in North Texas and in Kansas, they tended to section off large areas and put them to plow. Trail bosses had to find detours around these areas with increasing difficulty. The conflict would continue for more than a decade, finally making the Chisholm Trail impractical by the mid-1880s. During its time more than five million steers and another million horses had plodded up the Chisholm Trail—making it the site of the one of the largest movements of livestock in human history.

Western Trail

The Chisholm Trail would not be the only route to Kansas. John T. Lytle, a Pennsylvania-born entrepreneur, was responsible for starting the next major cattle route north. As a teenager, Lytle had moved to San Antonio with his family in 1860. He worked there as in the county clerk's office until he was forced to resign because of poor health. He moved to live on an uncle's ranch in Atascosa County, where the outdoor work and physical exercise improved his health. In 1863 he joined in the Thirty-Second Texas Cavalry and rose to the rank of sergeant by the end of the Civil War. He returned from the fighting to his uncle's ranch, but two years later decided to begin his own cattle outfit near Castroville.

Before long Lytle, like his contemporary Reynolds, discovered there would be money in moving cattle up the trails to market. Besides driving his own animals, Lytle served as a contract drover for his neighbors. He was wisely covering both ends of the business—he could earn a guaranteed amount based on the number of cattle he moved and not suffer as badly by price fluctuations in the market. In 1871 he formed a partnership with his cousin, Thomas M. McDaniel, near present day Lytle, Texas, and began to market his services to area ranchers. Over the next three years Lytle led several cattle drives to the northern rail heads in Kansas, but he pushed his cattle west of the more populated route of the Chisholm Trail. On one of his trips, as he passed through the Callahan Divide in Taylor County, he discovered a cove that was perfect for holding cattle. He developed the area as a place to stage and rest his herds before pushing farther up the trail. The cove and a nearby creek both bear his name.

As the era of the cattle drive advanced, more and more settlements in Kansas enticed Texas herds to their pens. Railroads pushed further onto the prairies, and villages leapfrogged west, each hoping to be the next boomtown. The threat of Indians and the presence of large, disruptive buffalo herds along the way caused few to follow Lytle's example at first, but by 1876 the Kiowas and Comanches had surrendered after the Red River War, and hunters rapidly annihilated the buffalo. The bulk of cattle traffic was free to move over to Lytle's Western, or Dodge City, Trail.

This new route soon eclipsed the Chisholm Trail. Originating in southern Texas, the Western Trail began with several feeder routes. All of them converged at Kerrville, then passed northward east of Brady. At Cow Gap, the trail picked up feeder trails from Mason, San Saba, and Lampasas and then passed through Coleman. There it picked up feeders from Trickham and Tom Green County. For the next several miles, the trail fanned out significantly for grazing purposes, with paths going through the sites of modern Putnam, Baird, and Clyde. Reuniting at Albany, the trail crossed the Clear Fork of the Brazos River near Fort Griffin. There, a second feeder from Tom Green County, which had gone through Buffalo Gap in Taylor County and across the site of present-day Abilene, joined the trail. The path headed northward through Throckmorton, then over the Brazos at Seymour, then, after crossing the Pease, it moved northwestward to enter Indian Territory at what would later be known as Doan's Crossing of the Red River. With several routes through the Indian Territory, the trail's ultimate terminus was Dodge City, Kansas.

Hired drovers like Lytle, and not the herd owners, were usually the hands that drove Texas herds up the trail. The cattle raisers usually remained home tending their breeding stock while trailing outfits charged $1 to $1.50 a head to get the animals safely to the pens and returned to the sponsoring ranch with the profits. Composed mostly of young men, many of whom had been hardened to outdoor living by service in the Confederate army, these operations often acquired cattle of their own and started such operations as the Cross Ell Ranch. The most famous of these contract cow handlers included John and William Blocker, George Littlefield, Ike Pryor, Moses Coggin, Eugene Millett, and William Jennings. Their success in business relied upon their ability to handle a sizable herd over long distances, sell for a good price, and do it all with the least amount of hands.

A typical outfit would be composed of up to a dozen herders. Two thirds of the people who trailed cattle out of Texas were white, but at least a third were either Hispanic, Indian, or African American. There were even a few women who endured the trek. Cowboys or "waddies" worked the herd, usually young men between twelve and twenty years old. Others found employment as wranglers among the *remuda*, some fifty horses that accompanied the cattle drive and served as remounts for use by the hands. These youngsters were supervised by "ramrods," seasoned trail veterans in their twenties. Older, more experienced men tended the chuck wagons as cooks or served the cattle raisers as trail bosses. This team was responsible for getting up to three thousand bawling, cantankerous, ornery beeves to market.

Wages were good for that day and offered an economic boost to men of modest means. Waddies could count on between $8 and $40 a trip while horse wranglers earned up to $50. Cooks and ramrods, with their experience and skill, could demand as much as $75. Trail bosses, with their keen eye for business, accounting sense, iron discipline, and steely focus on the job at hand fetched up to $100 in wages plus a percentage of the profits at trail's end.

A drive started with a roundup of existing herds or a cow hunt among the creek bottoms and thickets of frontier Texas. Once these animals were gathered, they were branded, doctored, and rested for the trip ahead. Often trail herds consisted of animals from several small ranches. Trail bosses advertised for hands, then hired the most promising buckaroos from among the applicants. Often these were first timers to such an adventure, but ramrods and cooks were highly sought after for their experience.

Once the drive commenced, the days followed each other for weeks on end with a monotonous regularity. First up each morning was the cook who served up a breakfast of staples like oatmeal, beans, and cornmeal mush. Strong black coffee was plentiful and scalding hot. After breakfast the hands rolled up their "hot sacks" or blankets and loaded them into the supply wagons to be transported to the next campsite, some ten or fifteen miles away. As the cowboys saddled their horses and prepared for another day's work, the cook would lead the wagons north, searching for the next spot of ground to call home. Behind him, a mile or so off, the wranglers would urge the remuda along. Once the cattle were roused and milling, the waddies would string the herd out into a slow-moving column of animals. To guide them, two or more hands would ride ahead of the herd on "point," along either side on "flank," or behind on "drag," — the least desired position due to the dust and smell churned up by several thousand cattle.

Despite the romantic image that surrounds the cowboy, little of his work was glamorous. Most days were boring, with hours on end being spent in the saddle under a bright, hot sky while the herd plodded along at a snail's pace, chewing up the prairie grass as they grazed their way to market, six to twelve weeks away. Night guard was a necessity, and the hands took turns staying mounted out among the sleeping cattle as the clear prairie nights drifted by. Even the Longhorns were rather coarse. Unlike the sleek, fat animals of eastern farms, these Texas range cattle were bony, gangly, and seemed all out of proportion, their hides scarred and mottled. Even so, they were a hardy if unlovely breed that not only stood the rigors of the trail, but actually thrived and gained weight as they walked their way to the railheads.

Occasionally, extreme terror punctuated this boredom. Thunderstorms would stampede the cattle or lightning might kill man and beast. Rivers could be swollen from rains or dry from drought. Hooves and horns were always potential killers, and the half-wild Longhorns could be unpredictable. Even a simple fall from a horse could prove fatal. There were also dangers from men. Indians, in their waning days as lords of the South Plains, might make forays against horse and cattle herds. At the occasional "Cow Towns" like Fort Worth or "Hell Towns" like Fort Griffin, gamblers, working women, and common bandits were ever eager to separate a cowboy from his money, his equipment, or even his life. Pistols, useful tools in directing and protecting herds, might become instruments of death in the hands of careless young men.

The Western Trail allowed significant growth in the Texas cattle industry in the years after the Civil War. By 1879 it was the most traveled of cattle drives. By 1885 nearly six million beeves had headed for America's heartland by following this trail. Those not destined for the dinner table were pushed on beyond Kansas to start new stock herds in Nebraska, the Dakotas, Colorado, Wyoming, and Montana. For most this was a chance to glimpse an untainted land that would hardly be recognizable a century later. "The year of 1877, we started a herd to Kansas. I routed right through Buffalo Gap, where Carter and Grounds had a little supply store and that was the whole town at the time," wrote cowboy Bob Lauderdale. "From there we went on by where the present town of Abilene [Texas] is located, but then that also was a bald prairie."

But the days of the trail drivers was nearing its end. Texas Fever scares reemerged, and a blizzard of quarantines and regulations followed. Frustrated, drovers and cattlemen lobbied Congress to create a national cattle highway that would run from the Nueces River to Canada, but the day and the mood had passed. The arrival of barbed wire on the prairies doomed the enterprise. Open range herders found themselves blocked from their traditional trails and waterholes. In addition, the progress of the railroad into western Texas made the trail obsolete. By the end of the 1880s, the way to Dodge City was increasingly difficult to navigate amid the legal, physical, and increasingly economic barriers. An American way of life, indelibly linked to the identity of this nation, was becoming extinct.

For those who had experienced it, the exciting days of their youth spent on the trail could never be matched. "I sometimes wonder if there ever was before, or has been since, any lure that equaled that of the cattle trail," remembered Jonathan M. Doak of his time as a cowboy. "I doubt there will ever be a venture fraught with more danger, privation and pleasure. Strange combination, isn't it?" A.D. Cantrell also had bitter-sweet memories of the trail-driving past. "Sometimes I get so homesick for the old days," he admitted late in life. "I shore would like to round up a few more thousand head of cattle and rope and brand and eat camp chuck. And drink hot black coffee with the boys. Yes sir, I shore would, and I'm not stuttering when I say it either."

J.R. Blocker, famous as one of the stalwarts among the old breed, knew that he and his comrades had participated in something profound to American history. "The ranks of the old trail drivers are becoming thinner each year, but there still remain many who knew the pleasures and hardships of a six and eight months' trip to market with from fifteen hundred to three thousand head of cattle," he wrote. "They are scattered from Texas to the Canadian border and from California to New York."

The boys of the 1870s had become the men of later years and had left their marks in dozens of different ways. "Many are rated in Dun and Bradstreet's in the seven-figure column, while others are not so well off financially," Blocker continued. "The stories some of these old fellows could tell would make your hair stand on end, stories of stampedes and Indian raids, stories with dangers and pleasures intermingled and of fortunes made and lost; they made history which the world does not know a thing about."

Chapter Seven
The Frontier Transformed

One day in the 1870s along the cattle trail, a group of cowboys came across a man trying to steal a portion of the herd. They knew that this type of activity was a common occurrence on the trail, but they were surprised to discover that they knew the man. He had been along on previous drives, and they had shared many meals together around the campfire. They invited the man to join them for supper. When all had their fill, the trail boss informed the man that they were now going to have to hang him. The man showed little surprise; in fact, he expected the outcome. Thinking quickly, he smiled at the men and said, "Boys, I'll not argue with you, I'll not deny my guilt or ask for mercy." Cleverly, he added: "I want at least one honest man to have a part in my hanging." As the cowboys looked on curiously and wondered what he meant, the man continued, "Now I want the one of you who never stole a cow to step forward and put the noose around my neck." The men stood in a silent state of shock for a few seconds, followed by uproarious laughter. They let him go with a warning.

Life was cheap on the frontier. The cattle drives may have changed the nature of the dangers there, but they also opened up the region to a wide new range of opportunities.

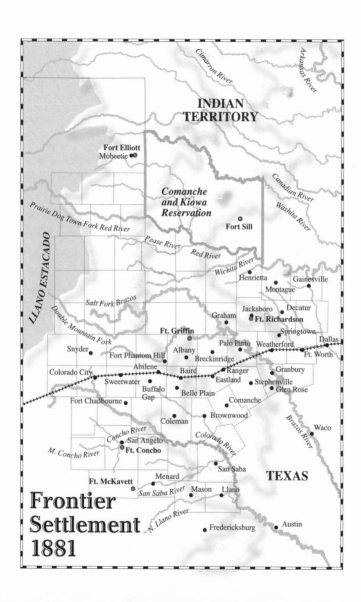

Frontier
Settlement
1881

These changes ranged from negative influences, such as the temptation to steal cattle, to the firm establishment of a new community of people creating a new permanence in the region.

Cattle Rustling

As long as there had been cattle on the Texas frontier, there had been the possible hazard of their theft. Early settlers often had to contend with Indians stealing parts of the herd. Indians more frequently targeted horses, but in times of short food supply they would drive off and butcher cattle. Indians would also drive off settlers' cattle in an effort to try to force them from hunting grounds.

The most common type of rustler was the experienced cowboy whose herding practices drifted toward the unethical and illegal. A common opportunity for any entrepreneurial young man was simply to buy a small herd, register a brand, and then begin to hunt and brand stray cattle on the open range. Claiming an unbranded steer as one's own was legal, unless it was clear that the animal was the calf of a clearly branded cow. Nevertheless, many rustlers began by culling out large unbranded calves from others' herds. Some got greedy and even began to seek calves that had not yet weaned. The problem with this practice was that Longhorn cows and calves have a strong natural urge to seek each other out if separated before the calf is weaned. In fact, many rustlers were discovered because they had stolen an unweaned calf, branded it with their own mark, only to find that the calf had left their enclosure and traveled for miles to find its mother. Seeing a calf with a different brand was often the tip off for ranchers that rustlers were in the area.

Rustlers came up with a variety of solutions to this problem. Some would keep stolen calves in a pen until they learned to eat grass, and only then would they brand them. The risk of this practice was that having a pen full of bawling, unweaned calves without their mothers looked awfully suspicious. Other solutions were more cruel: they would cut the muscles that operated the calf's eyelids, making the animal temporarily blind and, therefore, unable to return to its mother. Another option was to slit the calf's tongue down the middle so that the calf could not suckle and would have to wean to survive. A final solution was to kill the mother during the theft.

Formal prosecution of cattle rustlers was infrequent because most incidents occurred along the isolated cattle trails or in other areas of the open range. Most often, cattlemen took it upon themselves to dispense justice against rustlers. The amount of rustling would not begin to subside until the cattle drives came to an end and the region moved toward fenced ranches.

The Seedy Side of the Cattle Drives

The cattle kingdom brought large numbers of people to the Texas frontier, and with them came an increase in the variety and quantity of vices. Cow towns of varying sizes emerged along the cattle trails to provide a variety of services for the young cowboys whose day-to-day lives consisted normally of the monotony of the cattle trail.

Along both the Goodnight-Loving Trail and the Western Cattle Trail, the most influential—and most notorious—of these cow towns was known as the "Flats" adjacent to Fort Griffin. Built next to the fort at the Clear Fork of the Brazos crossing in Shackelford County, the Flats initially served as a civilian community to service the needs of the soldiers. The town also served as a major base for buffalo hunters in the mid-1870s. Once the great cattle drives began, however, the Flats developed into a wild town of drinking, gambling, prostitution, and other vices to tempt the lonely cowboys away from the trail.

One of the more celebrated images in the popular imagination about life on the frontier is that of the saloon table poker game. Professional gamblers did roam the region looking for a game and made their fortunes off of the unfortunate cowboy or buffalo hunter who came into their sights. Gambling was one of the prominent features of life on the Texas frontier. The practice had gotten its start even before the creation of towns and saloons, beginning with the early line of West Texas forts that came in the 1850s. Soldiers spent much of their "down" time gambling with each other. When cattlemen started to dot the plains, betting on horse races, or playing cards was a favorite pastime for their cowboys.

After the Civil War professional gamblers started to make their way into the region. They tended to travel a circuit, going from frontier town to frontier town, staying as long as they found lucrative action. Two of the more famous gamblers to have spent time in the region were "Doc" Holliday and Charlotte Thompkins, also known as "Lottie Deno—the Poker Queen." Gamblers could be found on any given day in the back of any saloon in the region.

Professional gamblers preyed on cowboys and buffalo hunters. Gamblers could take advantage of these men because of the circumstances of their particular professions. Both cowboys and buffalo hunters spent long weeks out on the plains with no entertainment or amusements outside of their work. And both groups got paid in lump sums at the end of their job. Gamblers flocked to these men like bees to nectar. Because officials did not closely regulate gambling, marked cards, loaded dice, and other methods of cheating were common. In describing the methods of the professional gamblers, one contemporary observer claimed, "The ordinary fellow did not have a ghost of a show." He elaborated: "I saw a buffalo hunter come to town one day and market his season's kill for $1,500." After a single night in the town with the gamblers, the next morning, this hunter "had to borrow money for his breakfast. The gamblers had gotten it all."

The transient nature of life on the frontier also helped prostitution to flourish in the region in the nineteenth century. Cowboys, buffalo hunters, and soldiers all created a demand, with prostitutes charging twenty-five cents to five dollars for their services. Buffalo Gap, Rath City, and "Hide Town" (now Snyder) all attracted the business because of the traffic in buffalo hunters. Saint Angela (now San Angelo) by

From the Collection of the Robert E. Nail Archives of the Old Jail Art Center, Albany, Texas

Drawing by Edgar Rye of Fort Griffin Military Post and Town as it appeared in 1876

Fort Concho also had a bustling "red-light district." Perhaps no place in the region, however, had a more extensive trade in prostitution than the Flats by Fort Griffin. The Flats had about two blocks of brothels extending down both sides of a main street.

In most of these towns, the women worked with the support of the local saloonkeepers and merchants. If one of the women found a particularly naive cowboy, she might take him around from store to store during the day, slowly milking him of every last cent, with the help of the storeowners.

Despite its obvious presence, prostitution was not a legal activity in the region. Prostitutes functioned at the mercy of the local law, and they knew that at any time they could fall out of favor with the powers that be and end up in jail or run out of town.

As more towns came to West Texas, and with them schools, churches, and families, the business of prostitution declined sharply. With a more stable population, the demand had decreased. Some of these new citizens let the soiled doves know that they disapproved of their profession. "Bad meat draws flies," read one hand-lettered notice tacked to one prostitute's shanty on the banks of the Clear Fork. This observation was followed by "Leave or you are doomed." In spite of this intimidation, the world's oldest profession never disappeared completely.

Crime, Violence, and Vigilante Justice

Other types of lawlessness also defined the post-Civil War frontier, including gunfights, made infamous by Hollywood in later generations. "A killing was one of the ordinary, expected events of the night," remembered pioneer R.A. Slack, "on which comments were over and the incident closed by the time the blood had been mopped up from the floor."

Perhaps the most dangerous gunman to have ever operated in Texas, John Wesley Hardin was a study in contrasts. He always considered himself a gentleman, who said he only ever killed to save his own life; but by the time of his death, he had killed more than forty men. Born in Bonham, Texas, on May 26, 1853, Hardin began with every prospect of leading a normal, prosperous life. His father, James G. Hardin, was a Methodist preacher, circuit rider, teacher, and lawyer. Nevertheless, young John Wesley (Wes) got into to trouble at an early age. At thirteen, he stabbed a classmate in a schoolyard fight. Two years later, he shot and killed a black man with whom he had argued. Texas's Reconstruction government issued a warrant for young Hardin's arrest, so he fled to his brother's house, twenty-five miles north of Sumpter, Texas. By 1869 Hardin had killed four soldiers who had come to arrest him.

Hardin decided to change his luck by becoming a cowboy. In 1871 he signed on with a cattle outfit heading up the Chisholm Trail toward Abilene, Kansas. This career change did not detain his deadly impulses. Hardin killed seven people along the trail and three people in Abilene. He even allegedly backed down Abilene, Kansas, city marshal Wild Bill Hickok.

Hardin returned to Gonzales County, where he met and married Jane Bowen, with whom he fathered three children. In the meantime, Governor Edmund J. Davis's State Police began to seek him actively for arrest. Hardin added four more victims to his death list before he surrendered to the Cherokee County sheriff in 1872. A month later he escaped and started raising cattle for himself.

In 1873-1874 West Texas became embroiled in the Sutton-Taylor Feud, which pitted anti-Reconstruction forces under Jim Taylor against former State Police forces affiliated with William Sutton. Hardin joined the Taylor faction and hunted down former State Police Captain Jack Helm and killed him in a blacksmith shop in Wilson County. When the feud ended in 1874, Hardin drove two herds of cattle up the Chisholm Trail, but even this could not keep him from violence. While visiting Comanche, Texas, he killed the deputy sheriff of Brown County, Charles Webb.

With this murder, Hardin became one of the most wanted killers in Texas history. He fled with his family to Alabama and Florida (killing as many as six more people along the way). The Texas Rangers tracked him to Florida and arrested him on July 23, 1877, bringing him back to Comanche to stand trial for Webb's murder. With a guilty verdict on September 28, 1878, the judge sentenced Hardin to twenty-five years in prison. While incarcerated, Hardin made the most of his time. Between repeated efforts at escape, he read books, was the superintendent of the prison Sunday school, and studied law. Upon his release in 1894, the State of Texas admitted John Wesley Hardin to the bar.

Despite efforts to become a decent, law-abiding citizen, Hardin ultimately fell back into old patterns. He moved to El Paso in 1895, opened a law practice, and took as a lover the wife of one of his clients, Martin Morose. When Morose discovered the affair, Hardin hired several law officials to kill the man. But on August 16, 1895, one of the hired assassins, Constable John Selman, demanded that Hardin pay him more money for the job. When Hardin refused, Selman

Certificate of Pardon for John Wesley Hardin. After fifteen years in prison for one of his forty-four murders, Hardin received this pardon.

opened fire on him in the Acme Saloon, killing him instantly. In the end John Wesley Hardin died the way he lived—violently.

Other killers on the frontier had to deal with a rise in vigilantism as citizens frustrated with lawlessness took responsibility for dispensing justice on their own. One case involved vigilantism but also created a real frontier mystery. James A. Brock, a native of Ohio, moved to West Texas with the vanguard of settlers in the mid-1870s. Before he left the region, he would be accused of cattle rustling and murder, and he would barely escape with his life in the face of a vigilance committee.

When Brock arrived in the region he went first to Fort Griffin, where he became a sutler's clerk. Contemporaries described him as a "high-hatter" and a "true gentleman." Brock soon came upon a plan to get into the cattle business. He offered to buy the stragglers from herds traveling through the area on their way north. This scheme proved successful, and soon Brock bought land south of the fort and sent for his two cousins, Frank and Ed Woosley, to help finance and run the ranch. Over the next year the Brock-Woosley Ranch enjoyed tremendous success.

Brock and the Woosleys soon started arguing over profits and shares in the ranch. People in the community watched this trouble boil up, and many openly predicted trouble. Then, on May 22, 1877, Frank Woosley vanished. That morning he was seen with two saddle horses, and he stopped at a local ranch to ask directions to the "cow outfit," and then he rode away. He was never seen again in West Texas.

When Woosley's extra horses were found walking back to Brock's ranch, area residents immediately assumed the worst. Suspicion fell on Brock—the logical choice, if someone had murdered Frank Woosley. The victim's brother, Ed, made that assumption, and he issued a $500 reward to anyone who would "find the body of my brother FRANK WOOSLEY, who is . . . supposed to have been murdered." Brock increased the suspicion against himself by offering a $1,000 reward of his own for the discovery of his cousin. That he was willing to risk so much convinced West Texans that he must *know* that Woosley would never be found.

Vigilantes tried to get Brock to confess to the murder through intimidation tactics. When that did not work, area ranchers brought suit against him for stealing cattle. Brock had to fight these charges in court for the next three years. Even though he won every decision, the long, drawn-out court battles ruined his business, and he eventually had to sell his ranch for $1,000, a tenth of its estimated worth.

Once Brock disengaged from the legal system, he embarked on an obsessive interstate search to find his cousin and clear his name. Adding to his $1,000 reward offer, Brock made cards with his cousin's description and distributed them to lawmen throughout the United States, Canada, and Mexico. No longer a rancher, Brock became a subcontractor on a six-hundred-mile U.S. Mail route so he could remain in contact with countless travelers.

Fourteen years after Frank Woosley disappeared, James Brock finally received the news he had been seeking. A

Georgia detective, G.B. Wells, had received one of Brock's cards. While searching for another man in Arkansas, Wells, by chance, recognized Woosley. He wired Brock: "Have one of your cards and am sure I have the man wanted." Brock desperately wired back: "When you are sure you have him located I will go for him. Don't arrest but keep spotted. . . . He is an infidel."

Brock joined Wells and a sheriff in Arkansas, and they caught a train, unaware that Woosley was also on board. At a stopover in Augusta, Arkansas, Brock recognized his cousin. With pistol in hand, Brock approached Woosley, while Wells and the sheriff closed in from behind. Shocked and bewildered, Woosley cooperated fully. When asked about his unexplained disappearance, he stated that he had simply been "depressed" when he left and decided not to come back. The people of Brock's hometown, London, Ohio, had been debating his guilt or innocence for nearly fifteen years, and Woosley agreed to accompany Brock back to Ohio to put this debate to rest. When they arrived in London, the people greeted Brock as a conquering hero. Observers noted Brock's reaction "at the hour of his final triumph," stating that "he was overcome with emotion and cried like a child." Like Woosley, Brock never returned to West Texas.

Despite Brock's innocence in the Woosley case, vigilance committees still emerged among the growing group of settlers in West Texas. The most infamous of these committees formed in the vicinity of Fort Griffin in the 1870s. Consisting of some of the area's most successful and powerful citizens,

this committee first became known as the Old Law Mob
(OLM), but it eventually came to be called the Tin Hat
Brigade.

Membership in the vigilante committees was secret, and
their tactics were unequivocal. The Tin Hat Brigade targeted
thieves in order to protect citizens' property. The group
would ride in the night wearing bandanas to cover their
faces, and they would surprise their suspect in his sleep. Most
commonly the next step was to execute the suspect by hanging him from a tree in a public area. This action would then
serve as a deterrent to other criminals. The vigilante movement did serve to deter some criminals, but it also brought
fear and intimidation to both the guilty and innocent. Most
of those visited by the committee probably had committed a
crime, but it is doubtful if that crime had met the legal
requirements to deserve punishment by death.

The Tin Hat Brigade finally fell apart when its leader, former Sheriff John Larn, was arrested for cattle theft and murder. Born in Alabama in 1849, Larn migrated west after the
Civil War. His goal was to join the growing ranks of cattlemen
enjoying tremendous economic opportunities in the region.
Larn, however, had a mean streak. In 1869 he killed a rancher in Colorado and probably killed a sheriff in Santa Fe, New
Mexico, before he made his way to Fort Griffin, Texas. His
reputation was that of a direct, forthright, and dangerous fellow. "I believe that if a man was to shoot me through the
heart," he once boasted, "I would kill that man before I died."
After two years there, rancher Bill Hays hired Larn as fore-

man of a cattle drive to Trinidad, Colorado. On the trip Larn allegedly killed two Mexicans and a shepherd.

In 1873 Larn first became involved in law enforcement. Back in Texas, Bill Hays's cattle outfit had been accused of cattle rustling. Larn led the charges, and he accompanied a posse and thirteen soldiers from Fort Griffin to Bush Knob, in Throckmorton County, where the Hays outfit had been holding up. Larn and his men killed every member of the Hays crew.

Shortly after this action, Larn join the Tin Hat Brigade of the Fort Griffin area, and he gained instant respectability in the community, even marrying Mary Jane Matthews, of the powerful Matthews cattle family. He used his newfound popularity to get elected sheriff of Shackelford County in 1876, and in this capacity, he headed a citizens' posse to wipe out a gang of outlaws west of Fort Griffin. With thirteen citizens and twenty soldiers, Larn headed toward the rustlers' hideout, just west of the Double Mountains. The group first found and killed the gang's lookout, "Larapie Dan" Moran. Then they chased down eight others. A few of the outlaws escaped, but those who did not were killed on the spot. "The best way to end" stock thefts, Sheriff Larn reportedly said to a companion, is "to end the thieves when caught." This statement would prove prophetic in Larn's life.

Larn resigned as sheriff in March 1877 after he had built a house on the Camp Cooper Ranch on the Clear Fork of the Brazos. One of the main reasons for his resignation, however, was the fact that Larn—along with an associate, John

Selman—had secretly established a network of cattle thieves. As long as he remained sheriff, his own cattle rustling ring would make him look bad. The citizens of Shackelford County, grateful for his law enforcement services, appointed Larn and Selman Deputy Inspectors of Hides and Animals. In this capacity, the two men could easily move cattle from other ranges to their own, and now the new sheriff would not have to worry about ranchers' complaints.

Local cattlemen grew suspicious when Larn gained some lucrative government beef contracts. He supplied Fort Griffin and the Tonkawa Indians with large amounts of beef, yet his herds never seemed to diminish and those around him kept losing cattle. Because he was still a prominent member of Shackelford society, and because of his position in the vigilance committee with other important residents, Larn enjoyed relative freedom to conduct his illicit affairs.

In 1878 the Texas Rangers began an investigation into Larn's practices. As evidence against Larn and Selman stacked up, many prominent citizens who had been part of the vigilance committee with Larn began to worry about their association with him. Some offered to help gather evidence, infuriating Larn. The Rangers moved in and arrested Larn and Selman and took them to Fort Griffin. Larn's connections with the fort, however, were too strong, and the judge released the men.

In June 1878 the Rangers struck a deal with Larn and Selman. The two men agreed to meet in early July and testify against the vigilance committee. On June 23, before the meeting could take place, Shackelford County Sheriff Bill Cruger obtained a warrant and arrived at Larn's ranch with a posse. Perhaps believing this to be part of his deal with the Rangers, Larn complied and handed over his weapons. When he discovered he was being taken to Albany rather than Fort Griffin, he began to tremble and curse. Upon arrival at Albany, the captors fitted Larn with shackles and placed him in the crude picket jail.

Larn would not live to see another day. That night, a group of men, draped with slickers and wearing bandanas over their faces, gathered at the jail. They approached the entrance and each of them emptied his gun into John Larn. The body of this lawman, rancher, outlaw, citizen was returned to his Camp Cooper Ranch and he was laid to rest next to his infant son.

With Larn's killing, the activities of the Tin Hat Brigade came under public scrutiny. Citizens were growing less inclined to allow their neighbors to dispense justice outside the confines of the regular law. Soon, vigilantism would be replaced by a more permanent law enforcement presence from the state. The *Fort Griffin Echo* expressed the mood of the local, permanent population when it spoke out against the criminal riff raff that drifted in and out of town. "Hang 'em first," wrote editor George W. Robson, "then if they persist in their innocent amusement, cremate them."

Social Life on the Frontier

A new wave of migration arrived in West Texas. Shopkeepers came to sell their wares to soldier, stockman, and settler. Purveyors of entertainment, comfort, and recreation followed. Contract buyers passed through to make their purchases of beef on the hoof before ordering them driven to market, which attracted cowboys, ranchers, and wranglers. Grocers and sellers of sundries trundled in to peddle their wares. And many of these citizens brought their wives and children who insisted upon such hallmarks of civilization as manufactured clothing, regular schools, and solid churches.

Sod dugouts and picket houses gave way to milled lumber and bricks as fortunes were made. Towns began to appear where none had existed before, some in the shadows of forts, others because the people had so ordained it. The one-time paramount fear of Indians seemed to fade, replaced by the fear of not making one's fortune in the face of such flush times.

As the frontier region of Texas began to transform after the Civil War, the area attracted more and more settlers from the East. "At the time, the name of Texas, more especially West Texas, was a synonym for lawlessness, desperadoes, and all that was wild and bad," recorded Sallie Reynolds Matthews, pioneer in Shackelford County. "There was also a leaven of good, those rugged self-disciplined pioneers, men and women of foresight and courage, who were willing to brave the dangerous unknown and undergo countless hardships and privations for the sake of widening their horizons and preparing an easier road for their children."

Conditions on the frontier fell heaviest on women. "I am lonesome, Oh: very lonesome," wrote Susan E. Newcomb about her life on the Clear Fork. "I actually think that it is almost a sin for a person to live here where they can scarcely ever see anyone, and are always lonesome. We have been living here over a year and there has been one woman to see us, only one." Sophie Poe, wife of a buffalo hunter, echoed this sentiment. "I felt as if I were alone on a vast sea," she wrote, "and wondered where my next harbor was going to be."

As more settlers moved onto the frontier of West Texas, many began to seek ways to alleviate the monotony of their rather isolated lives. Of course, most of their time was taken up by working the cattle, tending the gardens, and keeping house. Neighbors were almost instantly friends, and on an isolated homestead civility ruled. "We had no luxuries at that time, and while our homes and furniture were crude and rough, we were all like one family," wrote Mrs. J.J. Greenwood, a settler in Brown County. "Whatever we had we were willing to share with those less fortunate."

Even so, opportunities arose for a little enjoyment and West Texans found several avenues for amusement. A party was one of the most popular events for both men and women on the frontier. Social events often commemorated a holiday, like Christmas or Independence Day, but others were simply held to provide an opportunity for fellowship with area families. Invitations went out via word of mouth or through an announcement in the local newspaper. On the day of the event, families started out early. The goal was to get to the ranch or other site where the party was to be held by mid-afternoon, so they could water and feed the horses, eat supper, and get ready for the party. Each family usually brought food to be placed on a common table and served "covered-dish" style to one and all. The host usually provided a barbecued beef and other dishes to add to the feast. When the meal ended, the dancing begin, with a fiddler and a "caller" playing and calling waltzes, quadrilles, and schottisches until dawn. As the sun rose, the host would provide breakfast, and the sleepy guests would hitch up their wagons and start slowly back to their own ranches.

Another popular amusement for frontier settlers was horse racing. This activity drew people from long distances and proved to be one of the most natural sports for the area. Generally, two types of horse races existed in West Texas: the spontaneous, local race; and the big, advertised race. The local race occurred throughout the area, as individuals who were proud of their horse might challenge someone else to a race. These events drew instant spectators, but nothing compared to the larger, planned events. During the 1870s, the big races were quite popular and, for many, they were considered the event of the year. People would travel a hundred miles to witness such a race, which would usually take place in the late morning or early afternoon. Betting on the horses seemed to be a near universal practice, as was the consumption of alcohol throughout the day. Many ranches sent horses and riders to represent them in the races, lending to the festive spirit.

Wherever young men and women gathered, cupid was sure to show up. Settler W.J. Bryan seemed amazed at the transformation of many a tough cow hand into a girl-crazy dandy. "Why, the men all went calico minded as soon as they got a whiff of that Hoyt's cologne," he remembered, "and they swung those gals so fast that they got dust in their pockets."

Love leads to marriage, and another social high point on the frontier was weddings among settlers. Even though there were many more men than women on the West Texas frontier, weddings became a fairly common occurrence as cattle families moved into the region. Courtship usually lasted quite long, but once a couple became engaged, the wedding soon followed. The couple chose the date based on when the next preacher was scheduled to make his way into the region. In some cases, they even had to send to Weatherford or Fort Worth to bring a preacher to the area. The wedding invitation was a word-of-mouth announcement to everyone living within thirty or forty miles of the ranch.

On the wedding day, guests started arriving by late morning and filtered in throughout the early afternoon. Typically, settlers held the ceremony in the mid-afternoon on the front porch of the bride's parents' home, because there were usually too many people to fit inside. When the couple had finished saying their vows, guests lined up for congratulations, followed by a feast and a dance. The wedding feast was huge. The bride's family usually had been cooking for days, preparing hams, beef, cakes, pies, and other dishes. The meal could be served on make-shift tables outside, or on a single table

1876 wedding portrait of John Alexander Matthews and Sallie Ann Reynolds Matthews.

inside, with the guests being served in relays. After the feast, the party began with fiddles and other instruments leading the dance. Guests would dance and drink until dawn.

Guests rested briefly the next morning, but not for long, because they had to make their way to the "in-fair." This "in-fair" was a reception held at the groom's parents' house. The routine mirrored that of the previous day, with a big feast, followed by an all-night dance. A few nights after the wedding celebrations ended came the final ritual associated with frontier weddings—the charivari. The newlywed couples' close friends would plan this event in secret. On the appointed date, the friends would gather carrying horns, pots and pans, and other noise-making implements. They would stealthily make their way to the couples' house (usually around midnight) and, at a signal, make as much noise as possible. According to the custom, the couple could only stop the noise by inviting in the troupe and serving refreshments. Not all weddings on the frontier were this elaborate, but it is clear that frontier settlers valued the institution of marriage and the traditions of the wedding ceremony.

Of course, a more prevalent social activity than parties, horse races, or weddings was simply "visitin'." Ranch families would often travel to spend a week or two with friends or family at neighboring ranches. Women and children might make such trips alone when the men were away on cattle drives. During these visits, quilting, sewing, and cooking occupied the women, but they also enjoyed playing games, such as croquet, which had become a popular game in the region by the mid-1870s. Similarly, life at the various forts was also hard on women, and one officer's wife recalled that "nothing but stern necessity and duty took people to such a desolate place, so, when strangers did arrive, they were kindly welcomed and entertained."

God was never far from the mind of a pioneer—who more than likely needed all the allies he could get—and worship of a formal and informal nature helped create order out of the chaos of frontier living. Before the advent of the railroad into West Texas there was very little in the way of a permanent house of worship. Nevertheless, Protestant ministers made their way into the area alongside many of the other settlers.

Most ranch families followed a Protestant tradition in their faith. One of the first "communities" that afforded residents the opportunity to worship came with the citizen forts during the Civil War. The closeness with other families made worship a natural activity. Baptist ministers from Weatherford and Fort Worth made occasional trips to the area to preach.

When the war ended, the threat of Indian attacks continued to thwart the establishment of settlements and churches. When Throckmorton County rancher Flake Barber wanted to get married in 1868, he had to send to Weatherford for a preacher—a hundred miles to the east. A Rev. Clark, who was a Primitive (or "Hardshell") Baptist, was the only one who was willing to risk being attacked by Comanches or Kiowas. Rev. Clark believed that the region was religiously neglected, so he made monthly trips to the area thereafter, but he always traveled the hundred miles on foot, because he believed that there would be less danger with no horse to tempt the Indians.

Rev. Clark gained a reputation for bravery and devotion because of these journeys. This reputation was especially enhanced after one trip when a group of cowboys on one of the ranches along the way thought they would play a practical joke on the minister. The ranch hands left out early in the morning before Clark. They dressed as Indians and hid behind a hill, waiting to "ambush" the preacher and give him a fright. When Clark saw them, however, he knelt down, held up his Bible, and beckoned these "Indians" to come to him. The cowboys hung their heads in shame and stole away as quickly as they could.

As more families moved into West Texas in the 1870s, other ministers came with them. The Methodists were among the first to assign ministers to the region on a permanent basis, appointing Rev. Levi F. Collins to serve as missionary pastor to the region shortly following licensing him to preach in 1873. Collins organized several congregations in Callahan and Taylor Counties. He and rancher Sam Friend organized one Methodist Church called "Jim Ned" on the headwaters of Jim Ned Creek. For a short time, this congregation worshipped in a small cabin that still stands today at the Buffalo Gap Historic Village in Taylor County. Other Protestant ministers made their way into the region as well, but not in great numbers until after the entrance of the railroad, the influx of more settlers, and the establishment of towns.

Frontier Failures

By the late 1870s, with the threat of Indian attacks gone, many land promoters went to work trying to bring more settlers to West Texas. In the days before the railroad, few of these ventures met with much success. One such effort involved the Texas-Franco Land Company, which had bought several tracts of land in West Texas. In 1878 the company tried to entice two hundred Russian Mennonites to the center of Taylor County. The Russians sent an advance guard to inspect the site, and they determined that these immigrants could probably do better in Arkansas.

The Eagle Colony would have a more disastrous outcome. In the spring of 1878 a land promoter calling himself Coldwater convinced a group of German immigrants that West Texas was the promised land. These Germans, recently arrived in America, were working at the Studebaker Wagon Factory in South Bend, Indiana. Coldwater told them that for $250 per family, he would furnish wagons and mules, oversee the move from Indiana, and set them up in their new location.

Sixteen families handed over their life savings to Coldwater and began the long journey to West Texas. They traveled by train to Fort Worth, then by wagon through Weatherford, Breckenridge, and Fort Griffin to their final destination—Lytle Creek in Taylor County (in the southern part of modern-day Abilene). At first, the immigrants were convinced that West Texas was a paradise. The creek provided good water and had abundant fish, deer and other game crowded the area, and even their small gardens grew quickly in the first few weeks after their arrival. Delighted, the Eagle colonists started to lay out streets for a huge town and build picket houses and rock fences.

Then everything fell apart. Coldwater, who had been holding their life savings for safe keeping, disappeared with the money. The colonists believed they could push on, because at least they had new teams and wagons. They would be able to build up their community. But Coldwater had not even paid for their wagons—he had taken out a note, due in November 1878. The Taylor County Sheriff traveled from Buffalo Gap to the colony to foreclose the wagons and repossess them. A few colonists heard that the sheriff was on his way, and hid their wagons in the creek bed and covered them with brush. But most of them lost everything.

Without wagons or teams, crops failed. Then the winter arrived early. In the bitter cold, the colonists ran out of food; some of the children died of malnutrition. The Eagle colonists probably would not have survived the winter had it not been for several cattle outfits taking pity and providing them with food. Most of the Eagles left the area and moved back East. A few, however, remained, and would become some of the earliest families of Abilene when it was founded two years later.

Sometimes the elements alone conspired to drive away the timid. One West Texas dugout had a poignant epitaph scrawled in charcoal upon its leather hinged door. "Gone Back East to Wife's Family," it read, "20 miles to Water, 10 Miles to Wood, 6 Inches to Hell; Make Yourself at Home."

The land of the Texas frontier had been a magnet for human settlement for thousands of years and not all who came persisted. By 1880 a new order of things had emerged. The Indians who had lived nomadic lives, and the bison that sustained them, were no longer a presence on the frontier. White settlers had been trickling into the area for decades, living a hard-scrabble, conflict-filled life that was now transforming this new country into an established civilization like the one they had left.

This change would accelerate in the coming decades. Technology would ultimately defeat the old natural barriers of frontier Texas and allow families a comfortable, if not prosperous, life. The railroad had been the technological innovation that had energized the great cattle drives to Kansas. By 1880 the machines were inching their way into the Texas frontier. The Texas and Pacific Railroad stretched into the region once dominated by bison and Jumanos, then Apaches, Comanches, Kiowas, and others, conquering distance and time with ribbons of steel. Now the frontier was to be connected with the rest of the United States. The transformation was going to be complete.

Technology Conquers the Frontier

The coming of the railroad did not finish the frontier alone. Numerous factors enhanced this transformation as factories in the east, and the clever men who ran them, created new and innovative ways to make nature obey man, instead of vice versa. The cattle drives, perhaps the signature example of the efforts of simple men applying sheer brawn and hard work for great rewards, fell beneath this juggernaut of progress. The invention of barbed wire would doom the old merit system by which men long on adventure and imagination but short on hard capital could make a living by their wits and muscle. The open-range system of herding on the Texas frontier appeared to be a permanent fixture to those early opportunists who arrived to raise livestock. The idea of being able to fence in large acres on the vast prairies seemed impossible—not only did the land stretch out in all directions like a sea of grass, but also there were not nearly enough trees to build traditional fences of their eastern pasts.

But all of that changed in 1874. In November of that year, an Illinois man named Joseph Glidden received a patent for a fencing material consisting of a single strand of wire with wire barbs twisted in place every few feet. He called the pattern the "Winner," and it became the most commercially successful design of the hundred of different barbed wire patterns that eventually emerged.

The "Winner" became available in Texas in 1875, but there was little initial interest. In 1878, however, a San Antonio medicine show featured the design, inspiring John Warne "Bet-a-Million" Gates to demonstrate the product on San Antonio's Military Plaza by successfully fencing in a herd a wild Longhorns with a single strand. He advertised the barbed wire as "light as air, stronger than whiskey, and cheap as dirt." Sales exploded quickly, and barbed wire fences started to appear around the frontier.

Photograph of Cowboys on Roundup at X-Ranch, Albany, Texas, c. 1900s

Famed rancher and cattle driver Charles Goodnight would also play a major role in the growth of barbed wire on the frontier. He used it to fence off his grazing area in the Palo Duro Canyon, marking the range as reserved for his cattle alone. This practice spread quickly, changing forever the nature of the Texas cattle industry. Barbed wire fences grew around large areas of the prairie, cutting off trailing routes for other cattlemen. Despite continuing struggles punctuated by cutting fences and driving herds through others' land, the open range had come to an end.

Before the range could be fenced, though, there was another consideration. Water, heretofore the scarcest of West

Texas commodities, could also be tamed by the mass production of inexpensive windmills. Before windmills, there was no way to settle the vast, waterless areas of the region; people and livestock were tied directly to the various waterways that wound through the drought-prone plains. Now these same settlers and their animals could have water on demand. Windmills made it possible to pump groundwater, making a large portion of the region potentially productive.

Dutch and German immigrants to Texas built the earliest windmills in the European style, but these proved too bulky and impractical for the Texas frontier. In 1854, however, Daniel Halladay (Hallady or Halliday) of Connecticut built the first American windmill, mounted on a four-legged wooden tower that could be constructed in a day. The railroads were the first to recognize the utility of this invention, and they began to use windmills both as an inexpensive means to provide water for their steam engines and as a means of attracting potential settlers to areas where they intended to lay track.

Sheep rancher Christopher Doty conducted one of the first successful experiments with windmills. He moved his flock to Schleicher County and by 1882 his windmills provided all the water needed for his four thousand head of stock. Cattle ranchers followed suit and soon began using windmills throughout West Texas.

The windmill also created a variety of new jobs on ranches. One of the colorful characters who emerged on the plains with the windmill was the driller. He was usually a loner who followed the fence crews on a ranch in search of areas where he might find water. The driller would then bore a well with his horse-powered drilling rig.

Then came another character—the windmiller. Larger ranches employed several of these craftsmen, who set up the mills over the wells. They also traveled around the ranch, living in covered wagons, checking and repairing the windmills as they went. They would only see headquarters once or twice a month.

A third occupation was that of the range rider. Early windmills needed to be greased twice a week. The range rider crossed the plains carrying bottles of grease on his saddle. It was a dangerous job. When he arrived at a squeaking mill, he had to climb the tower, stop the rotation of the wheel with a pole until he could climb onto the platform, then let the wheel turn while he poured grease over it. To make matters worse, the windmill platform was often the only place for miles where wasps could build their nests. Range riders had to fight these wasps often, and more than one fell to their painful, lonely deaths in the process.

Because of the success of barbed wire and the windmill, settlement moved rapidly into the plains of West Texas. Ranches, and eventually cultivated fields, were the clear beneficiaries of this innovation. Like back East, capital once again ruled, and men with money controlled the land, and those without worked for those who did. Many lamented the passing of the old days. "We had been raised to run cattle on free grass, and Eastern capitalists coming in and buying up the land was a new one on us," wrote rancher William B.

Slaughter. Those who had ready cash, like Goodnight, made the change; others like Slaughter held out for a sliver of the old ways. "We moved our cattle further west," he explained. "Things were never the same any more after free range began disappearing." Rapidly, the freedom to make a future—the very essence of what had attracted people to the frontier in the first place—was, like a trail driver's campfire, flickering out before a new dawn breaking.

Within a half-dozen years, access to water and range, once considered basic to a person's rights in this area, were locked away forever under laws protecting private property. Now cattle could be fattened for market, and grass and water guaranteed. New breeds—Durhams and Herefords—arrived, their beefy sides replacing the bony profiles of the once-ubiquitous Longhorns. A new kind of ranching emerged, and most, but not all, of the brave souls who had toughed it out in the area were rewarded for their perseverance by owning title to their own land. Cattle now became a business like any other, and a poor landless man with half-wild Longhorns could no longer make a living at it. Some attempted to wage so-called fence cutting wars, but in the end, the day of the open range was done and Longhorns disappeared.

Technology had wrested the Texas frontier from nature. Feet, hooves, and wheels had crossed it, then rails and wires. Windmills and wells pumped life-giving water from its stony, subterranean prison beneath the prairie. Bullets had done their part as well. The greatest impact for frontier Texas, though, occurred in the dugout headquarters of John

Simpson's Hashknife Ranch in 1880. There, he and local ranchers S.L. Chalk, brothers John and Clabe Merchant, and John T. Berry, signed an agreement with representatives of the Texas and Pacific Railroad to bring that mighty engine of progress to the prairies of the frontier.

Within weeks, surveying crews divided forever the boundless range, laying out the straight path of the railroad. Just a few miles southeast of the dugout, along a new earthen berm soon to be topped with rails, workers with post and sledge drove a distance marker into the sod. This sign, bearing the inoffensive title of "Milepost 407," marked the heart of a railroad town destined to emerge on the plains the following year, a city called Abilene. On February 27, 1881, the first locomotive ran through the site. Lot sales for the new town, platted at 1,760 acres, would commence on March 15.

The process started by the application of barbed wire to the endless range of western Texas was perfected and finalized with the arrival of the railroad. Restricting the range, at first glance, seemed to deny the easy access to markets that trail driving had delivered. But in a strange duality, fenced ranching both attracted the rails and was made possible by the arrival of the railroads. Within a quarter century the process was nearly complete and western Texas was no longer a frontier, nor much of a boundary.

Frontier Texas had become another part of the nation. The arrival of reliable transportation would make the great American desert inhabitable. Climate and culture had been rendered a little less important, and such factors as the

Indians and the buffalo were memories. Their task complete, most forts closed in the 1880s, and social and settlement patterns began to resemble those further east. Cattle remained, but not like it had in the old days. The wide open spaces that were once the marvel of the newcomer now bore the faint trace of fences—the inevitable barrier of civilization. Even the old criteria for locating towns and other human settlement changed when the railroad arrived. Since nature could now be manipulated, it no longer dictated where a man lived. Instead, its conqueror, technology, made that decision. Old cow towns and buffalo camps, fort settlements and trading posts gave way to settled market communities, with rails passing near the downtown courthouse in a final reminder of the taming of western Texas.

Nearly a century after the founding of Abilene, one of its native sons captured the essence of the Texas frontier experience. "West Texas is at least as well defined by its attitudes as its statistics," writer A.C. Greene recorded in his poignant memoir, *A Personal Country*. "Perhaps my reasoning is tinctured by the old voices I hear from my youth, speaking through yellow-white mustaches and beards, talking contemptuously of people 'going back' to Sherman or Cleburne or Denton. 'Back' was another place, not 'here.' 'Going back' was defeat. It was giving up, selling out, letting something whip you instead of dying before you would admit you were whipped. And when they 'went back' it caused them to creep away in the night, leaving an empty cabin or a string of unpaid bills. The old-timers were proud they had been able to hang on, regardless of what shape they were in, 'here' where things were tough.

"Survival was their criterion."

Bibliography

General Reference

Conger, Roger N., et al. *Frontier Forts of Texas*. Waco: Texian Press, 1966.

Fehrenbach, T.R. *Lone Star: A History of Texas and the Texans*. New York: American Legacy Press, 1983.

Heitman, Francis B. *Historical Register and Dictionary of the United States Army from its Organization, September 29, 1789, to March 2, 1903*. 2 vols., Washington: GPO, 1903; rpt., Urbana: University of Illinois Press, 1965.

Nunley, Parker. *A Field Guide to Archeological Sites in Texas*. Austin: Texas Monthly Press, 1989.

Richardson, Rupert N., Adrian Anderson, and Ernest Wallace. *Texas: The Lone Star State*. Sixth Ed. Englewood Cliffs, N.J.: Prentice Hall, 1993.

Roberts, Robert B. *Encyclopedia of Historic Forts: The Military, Pioneer, and Trading Posts of the United States*. New York: Macmillan, 1988.

Smith, Thomas T. *The Old Army in Texas: A Research Guide to the U.S. Army in Nineteenth-Century Texas*. Austin: Texas State Historical Association, 2000.

Tyler, Ron, et al. *The New Handbook of Texas*. 6 vols. Austin: Texas State Historical Association, 1996.

Wooten, Dudley Goodall, ed. *A Comprehensive History of Texas*. 2 vols., Dallas: Scarff, 1898; rpt., Austin: Texas State Historical Association, 1986.

Published Primary Sources

Biggers, Don Hampton. *Shackelford County Sketches*. Albany, Texas: Albany News Office, 1908; rpt., ed. Joan Farmer, Albany and Fort Griffin, Texas: Clear Fork Press, 1974.

Carter, W.H. *From Yorktown to Santiago with the Sixth U.S. Cavalry*. Austin: State House Press, 1989.

Cook, John R. *The Border and the Buffalo: An Untold Story of the Southwest Plains*. Topeka, Kansas: Crane, 1907; rpt., Austin: State House Press, 1989.

Duff, Katharyn, ed. *Pioneer Days, Two Views: Early Days in West Texas and Recollections on Miss Tommie Clack*. Abilene: Zachry and Associates, 1979.

Friend, Llerena, ed. *M.K. Kellogg's Texas Journal, 1872*. Austin: University of Texas Press, 1967.

Gallaway, B. P., ed. *Texas, the Dark Corner of the Confederacy: Contemporary Accounts of the Lone Star State in the Civil War*. 3rd ed. Lincoln and London: University of Nebraska Press, 1994.

Gilmore, Kathleen. *A Documentary and Archaeological Investigation of Presidio de San Luis de las Amarillas and Mission Santa Cruz de San Sabá*. Austin: State Building Commission, 1967.

Hardin, John Wesley. *The Life of John Wesley Hardin As Written by Himself*. Seguin, Texas: Smith and Moore, 1896; new ed., Norman: University of Oklahoma Press, 1961.

Hornaday, William Temple. *The Extermination of the American Bison*. Washington: Government Printing Office, 1889.

Hughes, Stella. *Hashknife Cowboy: Recollections of Mack Hughes*. Tucson: University of Arizona Press, 1984.

John, Elizabeth A.H., and Adán Benavides, Jr., "Inside Comanchería, 1785: The Diary of Pedro Vial and Francisco Xavier Chaves." *Southwestern Historical Quarterly* 98 (July 1994).

Matthews, Sallie Reynolds. *Interwoven: A Pioneer Chronicle*. 4th ed. College Station: Texas A&M University Press, 1982.

McCoy, Joseph G. *Historic Sketches of the Cattle Trade of the West and Southwest*. Kansas City, Missouri: Ramsey, Millett, and Hudson, 1874; rpt., Philadelphia: Porcupine, 1974.

Nathan, Paul D., trans., and Lesley Byrd Simpson, ed. *The San Sabá Papers*. San Francisco: Howell, 1959.

Nimmo, Joseph, Jr. *Report in Regard to the Range and Cattle Business of the United States*. Washington: GPO, 1885; rpt., New York: Arno Press, 1972.

Ormsby, Waterman L. *The Butterfield Overland Mail*. San Marino, CA: Huntington Library, 1942.

Parker, William B. *Notes Taken during the Expedition Commanded by Capt. R.B. Marcy*. Austin: Texas State Historical Association, 1984.

Poe, Sophie A. *Buckboard Days*. Caldwell, Idaho, 1936; rpt., Albuquerque: University of New Mexico Press, 1981.

Thompson, Richard A. *Crossing the Border with the 4th Cavalry: Mackenzie's Raid into Mexico, 1873*. Waco, Tex.: Texian Press, 1986.

Wallace, Ernest, and David M. Vigness, eds. *Documents of Texas History*. Austin: Steck, 1963.

Wilbarger, J.W. *Indian Depredations in Texas*. Austin: Hutchings, 1889; rpt., Austin: State House Press, 1985.

Books

Adams, Effie Kaye. *Tall Black Texans: Men of Courage*. Dubuque, Iowa: Kendall-Hunt, 1972.

_____. *The Afro-American Texans*. San Antonio: University of Texas Institute of Texan Cultures, 1975.

Anderson, Charles G. *In Search of the Buffalo: The Story of J. Wright Mooar*. Seagraves, Texas: Pioneer, 1974.

Baker, T. Lindsay, and Billy R. Harrison. *Adobe Walls: The History and Archaeology of the 1874 Trading Post*. College Station: Texas A&M University Press, 1986.

Barr, Alwyn. *Black Texans: A History of Negroes in Texas, 1528-1971*. Austin: Jenkins, 1973.

Biggers, Don H. *Buffalo Guns and Barbed Wire*. 1902; rpt. Lubbock: Texas Tech University Press, 1991.

Billington, Ray Allen, and Martin Ridge. *Westward Expansion: A History of the American Frontier*. 5th ed. New York: The Macmillan Co., 1982.

Blanton, Joseph Edward. *John Larn*. Venture Press, 1994.

Branch, Hettye Wallace. *The Story of "80 John"*. New York: Greenwich, 1960.

Buckley B. Paddock, ed. *A Twentieth Century History and Biographical Record of North and West Texas*. Chicago: Lewis, 1906.

Butler, Anne M. *Daughters of Joy, Sisters of Mercy: Prostitutes in the American West, 1865-1890*. Urbana: University of Illinois Press, 1985.

Caldwell, Clifton. *Fort Davis: A Family Frontier Fort*. Albany, Tex.: Clear Fork Press, 1986.

Cantrell, Gregg. *Stephen F. Austin: Empresario of Texas*. New Haven: Yale University Press, 1999.

Capps, Benjamin. *The Warren Wagontrain Raid*. New York: The Dial Press, 1974.

Carlson, Paul H. *Texas Woolybacks: The Range Sheep and Goat Industry*. College Station: Texas A&M University Press, 1982.

Carroll, John M. *The Black Military Experience in the American West*. New York: Liveright, 1971.

Carter, Robert G. *On the Border with Mackenzie, or Winning West Texas from the Comanches*. Washington: Eynon Printing, 1935.

Cashion, Ty. *A Texas Frontier: The Clear Fork Country and Fort Griffin, 1849-1887*. Norman and London: University of Oklahoma Press, 1996.

Castañeda, Carlos E. *Our Catholic Heritage in Texas*. 7 vols. Austin: Von Boeckmann-Jones, 1936-58; rpt., New York: Arno, 1976.

Chrisman, Brutus Clay. *Early Days in Callahan County*. Abilene, Texas: Abilene Printing and Stationery, 1966.

Christian, Garna L. *Black Soldiers in Jim Crow Texas, 1899-1917*. College Station: Texas A&M University Press, 1995.

Clayton, Lawrence, and Joan Halford Farmer, eds. *Tracks Along the Clear Fork: Stories from Shackelford and Throckmorton Counties*. Abilene: McWhiney Foundation Press, 2000.

Clifton, Robert T. *Barbs, Prongs, Points, Prickers, and Stickers*. Norman: University of Oklahoma Press, 1970.

Conkling, Roscoe P. and Margaret B. *The Butterfield Overland Mail, 1857-1869*. 3 vols. Glendale, California: Clark, 1947.

Corwin, Hugh. *The Kiowa Indians: Their History and Life Stories*. Lawton, Oklahoma, 1958.

Crawford, Ann Fears, and Crystal Sasse Ragsdale. *Texas Women: Frontier to Future*. Austin: State House Press, 1998.

Crouch. Carrie J. *A History of Young County, Texas*. Austin: Texas State Historical Association, 1956.

Dale, Edward Everett. *The Range Cattle Industry*. Norman: University of Oklahoma Press, 1930.

Dary, David A. *The Buffalo Book*. Athens, Ohio: Swallow, 1974.

DeArment, Robert K. *Bravo of the Brazos: John Larn of Fort Griffin, Texas*. Norman: University of Oklahoma Press, 2002.

DeShields, James T. *Border Wars of Texas*. 1912; rpt. Austin: State House Press, 1993.

_____. *Cynthia Ann Parker: The Story of Her Capture*. Dallas, TX: Chama Press, 1991.

Dobie, J. Frank. *The Longhorns*. Boston: Little, Brown, 1941; rpt., Austin: University of Texas Press, 1980.

Donovan, Frank, and John Leeds Kerr. *Destination Topolobampo: The Kansas City, Mexico & Orient Railway*. San Marino, CA: Golden West, 1968.

Douglas, C.L. *Cattle Kings of Texas*. Rpt. Austin: State House Press, 1989.

_____. *The Gentlemen in the White Hats*. 1934; rpt. Austin: State House Press, 1992.

Drago, Harry S. *Great American Cattle Trails*. New York: Dodd, Mead, 1965.

Duff, Kathryn. *Abilene . . . On Catclaw Creek: A Profile of a West Texas Town*. Abilene: The Reporter Publishing Company, 1969.

Dunlay, Thomas W. *Wolves for the Blue Soldiers: Indian Scouts and Auxiliaries with the United States Army*. Lincoln: University of Nebraska Press, 1982.

Dykstra, Robert R. *The Cattle Towns*. New York: Alfred A. Knopf, 1968.

Fehrenbach, T.R. *Comanches: The Destruction of a People*. New York: Knopf, 1974.

Ferguson, John C. *Texas Myths and Legends: Stories of the Frontier*. Abilene: McWhiney Foundation Press, 2003.

Ford, Gus L. ed. *Texas Cattle Brands*. Dallas: Cockrell, 1936.

Foster, Morris W. *Being Comanche: A Social History of an American Indian Community*. Tucson: University of Arizona Press, 1991.

Gard, Wayne. *Cattle Brands of Texas*. Dallas: First National Bank, 1956.

_____. *The Chisholm Trail*. Norman: University of Oklahoma Press, 1954.

_____. *The Great Buffalo Hunt*. New York: Knopf, 1959.

Garretson, Martin S. *The American Bison*. New York: New York Zoological Society, 1938.

Green, A.C. *A Personal Country*. New York: Knopf, 1969.

Hacker, Margaret S. *Cynthia Ann Parker: The Life and the Legend*. El Paso, TX: Texas Western Press, 1990.

Hafen, LeRoy R. *Overland Mail, 1849-1869*. Cleveland: Clark, 1926.

Hagan, William T. *Quanah Parker, Comanche Chief*. Norman: University of Oklahoma Press, 1993.

_____. *United States-Comanche Relations: The Reservation Years*. New Haven: Yale University Press, 1976; rpt., Norman: University of Oklahoma Press, 1990.

Haley, J. Evetts. *Charles Goodnight*. Norman: University of Oklahoma Press, 1949.

_____. *Fort Concho and the Texas Frontier*. San Angelo, Tex.: San Angelo *Standard-Times*, 1952.

_____. *Southwestern Trails*. San Angelo, Tex.: San Angelo *Standard Times*, 1948.

_____. *The Heraldry of the Range: Some Southwestern Brands*. Canyon, Texas: Panhandle-Plains Historical Society, 1949.

_____. *The XIT Ranch of Texas and the Early Days of the Llano Estacado*. Chicago: Lakeside, 1929; rpt., Norman: University of Oklahoma Press, 1953, 1967.

Haley, James L. *The Buffalo War: The History of the Red River Indian Uprising of 1874*. Garden City, N.Y.: Doubleday, 1976; rpt. Austin: State House Press, 1998.

Hamilton, Allen Lee. *Sentinel of the Southern Plains: Fort Richardson and the Northwest Texas Frontier, 1866-1878*. Fort Worth: Texas Christian University Press, 1988.

Hays, Dick. *Windmills and Pumps of the Southwest*. Austin: Eakin Press, 1983.

Haywood, C. Robert. *Trails South: The Wagon-Road Economy in the Dodge City-Panhandle Region*. Norman: University of Oklahoma Press, 1986.

Hickerson, Nancy Parrott. *The Jumanos: Hunters and Traders of the South Plains*. Austin: University of Texas Press, 1994.

Holden, Frances Mayhugh. *Lambshead Before Interwoven: A Texas Range Chronicle, 1848-1878*. College Station: Texas A&M University Press, 1982.

Holden, William Curry. *Alkali Trails: Or Social and Economic Movements of the Texas Frontier, 1846-1900*. N.p: The Southwest Press, 1930; Rpt. Lubbock: Texas Tech University Press, 1998.

Hollon, W. Eugene, *Beyond the Cross Timbers: The Travels of Randolph B. Marcy,1812-1887*. Norman: University of Oklahoma Press, 1955.

_____. *Frontier Violence: Another Look*. New York: Oxford University Press, 1974.

Hunter, J. Marvin. *Trail Drivers of Texas*. 2 vols. 4th ed., Austin: University of Texas Press, 1985.

Hutton, Paul Andrew. *Phil Sheridan and His Army*. Lincoln: University of Nebraska Press, 1985.

Jackson, Jack. *Los Mesteños: Spanish Ranching in Texas, 1721-1821*. College Station: Texas A&M University Press, 1986.

John, Elizabeth. *Storms Brewed in Other Men's Worlds: The Confrontation of Indians, Spanish, and French in the Southwest, 1540-1795*. College Station: Texas A&M University Press, 1975.

Johnston, W.P. *The Life of Gen. Albert Sidney Johnston*. 1878; rpt. Austin: State House Press, 1997.

Jordan, Terry G. *North American Cattle-Ranching Frontiers*. Albuquerque: University of New Mexico Press, 1993.

_____. *Trails to Texas: Southern Roots of Western Cattle Ranching*. Lincoln: University of Nebraska Press, 1981.

Kavanagh, Thomas W. *Comanche Political History: An Ethnohistorical Perspective, 1706-1875*. Lincoln: University of Nebraska Press, 1995.

Kenner, Charles Leroy. *A History of New Mexican-Plains Indian Relations*. University of Oklahoma Press, 1969.

Kirkland, Forrest, and W. W. Newcomb, Jr. *The Rock Art of Texas Indians*. Austin: University of Texas Press, 1967.

Ledbetter, Barbara Neal. *Fort Belknap Frontier Saga: Indians, Negroes and Anglo-Americans on the Texas Frontier*. Burnet, Texas: Eakin Press, 1982.

Leckie, William H. *The Military Conquest of the Southern Plains*. Norman: University of Oklahoma Press, 1963.

Lomax, John A. and Alan. *Best Loved American Folk Songs*. New York: Groset and Dunlap, 1947.

Loomis, Noel M, and Abraham P. Nasatir. *Pedro Vial and the Roads to Santa Fe*. Norman: University of Oklahoma Press, 1967.

Mackey, Thomas C. *Red Lights Out: A Legal History of Prostitution, Disorderly Houses, and Vice Districts, 1870-1917*. New York: Garland, 1987.

Martin, Jack. *Border Boss: Captain John R. Hughes, Texas Ranger*. Austin: State House Press, 1990.

Mayhall, Mildred P. *The Kiowas*. Norman: University of Oklahoma Press, 1962; 2d ed. 1971.

McCallum, Henry D., and Frances T. McCallum. *The Wire That Fenced the West*. Norman: University of Oklahoma Press, 1965.

McConnell, Joseph Carroll. *West Texas Frontier*. Vol. 1, Jacksboro, Texas, 1933; Vol. 2, Palo Pinto, Texas, 1939.

McWhiney, Grady. *Cracker Culture: Celtic Ways in the Old South*. Tuscaloosa: University of Alabama Press, 1988.

Menard County Historical Society, *Menard County History: An Anthology*. San Angelo: Anchor, 1982.

Merrill, James M. *Spurs to Glory: The Story of the U.S. Cavalry*. Chicago: Rand McNally, 1966.

Metz, Leon C. *John Selman*. New York: Hastings House, 1966; 2d ed., Norman: University of Oklahoma Press, 1980.

Moore, Stephen L. *Taming Texas: Captain William T. Sadler's Lone Star Service*. Austin: State House Press, 2000.

Murrah, David J. *C.C. Slaughter: Rancher, Banker, Baptist*. Austin: University of Texas Press, 1981.

Myres, Sandra L. *The Ranch in Spanish Texas, 1691-1800*. El Paso: Texas Western Press, 1969.

Neighbours, Kenneth F. *Indian Exodus: Texas Indian Affairs, 1835-1859*. San Antonio: Nortex, 1973.

_____. *Robert Simpson Neighbors and the Texas Frontier, 1836-1859*. Waco: Texian Press, 1975.

Newcomb, William W. *The Indians of Texas*. Austin: University of Texas Press, 1961.

Nordyke, Lewis. *Great Roundup: The Story of Texas and Southwestern Cowmen*. New York: Morrow, 1955.

Nye, Wilbur Sturtevant. *Bad Medicine and Good: Tales of the Kiowas*. Norman: University of Oklahoma Press, 1962.

_____. *Carbine and Lance: The Story of Old Fort Sill*. Norman: University of Oklahoma Press, 1937.

Parsons, Chuck. *The Capture of John Wesley Hardin*. College Station, Texas: Creative Publishing, 1978.

Parsons, Chuck, and Marianne E. Hall Little. *Captain L.H. McNelly, Texas Ranger: The Life and Times of a Fighting Man*. Austin: State House Press, 2001.

Perkins, Doug. *Brave Men and Cold Steel: A History of Range Detectives and Their Peacemakers*. Fort Worth: Texas and Southwestern Cattle Raisers Foundation, 1984.

Pierce, Michael D. *The Most Promising Young Officer: A Life of Ranald Slidell Mackenzie*. Norman: University of Oklahoma Press, 1993.

Pritchett, Jewell G. *From the Top of Old Hayrick: A Narrative History of Coke County*. Abilene, Tex.: Pritchett, 1980.

Rath, Ida Ellen. *The Rath Trail*. Wichita, Kansas: McCormick-Armstrong, 1961.

Rathjen, Frederick W. *The Texas Panhandle Frontier*. Austin: University of Texas Press, 1973.

Richardson, Rupert N. *The Comanche Barrier to South Plains Settlement*. Glendale, California: Clark, 1933; rpt., Millwood, New York: Kraus, 1973.

_____. *The Frontier of Northwest Texas, 1846 to 1876*. Glendale, CA: Clark, 1963.

Rister, Carl Coke. *Robert E. Lee in Texas*. Norman: University of Oklahoma Press, 1946.

_____. *Fort Griffin on the Texas Frontier*. Norman: University of Oklahoma Press, 1956.

Rodenberger, Lou, ed. *31 by Lawrence Clayton*. Abilene: McWhiney Foundation Press, 2002.

Robinson, Charles M. III. *Bad Hand: A Biography of General Ranald S. Mackenzie*. Austin, Tex..: State House Press, 1993.

_____. *Indian Trial: The Complete Story of the Warren Wagon Train Massacre and the Fall of the Kiowa Nation*. Spokane, WA: Arthur H. Clark Co., 1997.

_____. *Satanta: The Life and Death of a War Chief*. Austin: Sate House Press, 1997.

Rogers, Model. *Old Ranches of the Texas Plains*. College Station: Texas A&M University Press, 1976.

Rose, Cynthia. *Lottie Deno: Gambling Queen of Hearts*. Santa Fe, New Mexico: Clear Light, 1994.

Rouse, John E. *The Criollo: Spanish Cattle in the Americas*. Norman: University of Oklahoma Press, 1977.

Rye, Edgar. *The Quirt and the Spur: Vanishing Shadows of the Texas Frontier*. Chicago: Conkey, 1909; facsimile ed., Austin: Steck-Vaughn, 1967.

Simpson, Harold B. *Cry Comanche: The Second U.S. Cavalry in Texas*. Hillsboro, TX: Hill Junior College Press, 1979.

Skaggs, Jimmy M. *Prime Cut: Livestock Raising and Meatpacking in the United States, 1607-1983*. College Station: Texas A&M University Press, 1986.

_____. *The Cattle-Trailing Industry: Between Supply and Demand, 1866-1890*. Lawrence: University Press of Kansas, 1973.

Smith, F. Todd. *The Caddos and Wichitas*. College Station: Texas A&M University Press, 1998.

Smith, Thomas T. *The U.S. Army and the Texas Frontier Economy, 1845-1900*. College Station: Texas A&M University Press, 1999.

Turner, Frederick Jackson. *The Frontier in American History*. 1947; rpt. Tucson: University of Arizona Press, 1986.

Utley, Robert M. *Frontier Regulars: The United States Army and the Indian, 1866-1891*. New York: Macmillan, 1973.

_____. *The Indian Frontier of the American West 1846-1890*. Albuquerque: University of New Mexico Press, 1984.

Wallace, Ernest, and E. Adamson Hoebel. *The Comanches*. Norman: University of Oklahoma Press, 1952.

Wallace, Ernest. *Ranald S. Mackenzie on the Texas Frontier*. Lubbock: West Texas Museum Association, 1964; rpt., College Station: Texas A&M University Press, 1993.

Ward, Hortense Warner. *Cattle Brands and Cow Hides*. Dallas: Story Book Press, 1953.

Webb, Walter Prescott. *The Great Plains*. Boston: Ginn, 1931.

_____. *The Great Frontier*. Lincoln: University of Nebraska Press, 1952.

_____. *The Texas Rangers*. Boston: Houghton Mifflin, 1935; rpt., Austin: University of Texas Press, 1982.

Weber, David J., ed. *New Spain's Far North Frontier: Essays on Spain in the American West, 1540-1821*. Albuquerque: University of New Mexico Press, 1984.

Weddle, Robert S. *The San Sabá Mission*. Austin: University of Texas Press, 1964.

Wellman, Paul I. *Death on the Prairie: The Thirty Years' Struggle for the Western Plains*. New York: Macmillan, 1934.

Weslager, C.A. *The Delaware Indians: A History*. Rutgers University Press, 1972.

Weston, Jack. *The Real American Cowboy*. New York: Schocken Books, 1985.

Wilkins, Frederick. *Defending Borders: The Texas Rangers, 1848-1861*. Austin: State House Press, 2001.

_____. *The Law Comes to Texas: The Texas Rangers, 1870-1901*. Austin: State House Press, 1999.

_____. *The Legend Begins: The Texas Rangers, 1823-1845*. Austin: State House Press, 1996.

Williams, Clayton W. *Texas' Last Frontier: Fort Stockton and the Trans-Pecos, 1861-1895*. College Station: Texas A&M University Press, 1982.

Winsor, Bill. *Texas in the Confederacy*. Hillsboro, Texas: Hill Junior College Press, 1978.

Wolfenstine, Manfred R. *The Manual of Brands and Marks*. Norman: University of Oklahoma Press, 1970.

Wooster, Robert. *The Military and United States Indian Policy, 1865-1903*. New Haven: Yale University Press, 1988.

_____. *Nelson A. Miles and the Twilight of the Frontier Army*. Lincoln: University of Nebraska Press, 1993.

_____. *Soldiers, Sutlers, and Settlers: Garrison Life on the Texas Frontier*. College Station: Texas A&M University Press, 1987.

Worcester, Donald E. *The Chisholm Trail*. Lincoln: University of Nebraska Press, 1980.

_____. *The Texas Longhorn: Relic of the Past, Asset for the Future*. College Station: Texas A&M University Press, 1987.

Zachry, Juanita Daniel. *The Settling of a Frontier: A History of Rural Taylor County*. Burnet, Tex: Nortex Press, 1980.

Articles

Anderson, H. Allen. "The Delaware and Shawnee Indians and the Republic of Texas, 1820-1845." *Southwestern Historical Quarterly* 94 (October 1990).

Bolton, Herbert E. "The Jumano Indians in Texas, 1650-1771." *Quarterly of the Texas State Historical Association* 15 (July 1911).

Crane, R.C. "D.W. Wallace (`80 John'): A Negro Cattleman on the Texas Frontier." *West Texas Historical Association Year Book* 28 (1952).

Crimmins, Martin L. "Fort McKavett, Texas," *Southwestern Historical Quarterly* 38 (July 1934).

_____. "Experiences of an Army Surgeon at Fort Chadbourne." *WestTexas Historical Association Year Book*, 15 (Oct., 1939), 31-39.

Day, James M. "A Preliminary Guide to the Study of Buffalo Trails in Texas," *West Texas Historical Association Year Book* 36 (1960).

Dunn, William E. "The Apache Mission on the San Saba River: Its Founding and Failure." *Southwestern Historical Quarterly* 17 (April 1914).

Gard, Wayne. "Retracing the Chisholm Trail." *Southwestern Historical Quarterly* 60 (July 1956).

_____. "The Mooar Brothers: Buffalo Hunters." *Southwestern Historical Quarterly* 63 (July 1959).

_____. "The Shawnee Trail." *Southwestern Historical Quarterly* 56 (January 1953).

Godbold, Mollie Moore. "Comanche and the Hardin Gang." *Southwestern Historical Quarterly* 67 (July, October 1963).

Haley, J. Evetts. "Texas Fever and the Winchester Quarantine." *Panhandle-Plains Historical Review* 8 (1935).

_____. "The Comanchero Trade." *Southwestern Historical Quarterly* 38 (January 1935).

Harmon, George D. "The United States Indian Policy in Texas, 1845-1860." *Mississippi Valley Historical Review* 17 (1930).

Havins, Thomas R. "The Texas Mounted Regiment at Camp Colorado," *Texas Military History* 4 (Summer 1964).

Holden, William Curry. "Frontier Defense in Texas during the Civil War." *West Texas Historical Association Year Book* 4 (1928).

Housely, Marilynne. "Forting Up on the Texas Frontier during the Civil War." *West Texas Historical Association Year Book* 17 (1941).

Hughes, Jack T. "Prehistoric Cultural Developments on the Texas High Plains." *Bulletin of the Texas Archeological Society* 60 (1989).

Humphrey, David C. "Prostitution in Texas: From the 1830s to the 1960s." *East Texas Historical Journal* 33 (1995).

Kelley, J. Charles. "Juan Sabeata and Diffusion in Aboriginal Texas." *American Anthropologist* 57 (October 1955).

Kincaid, Naomi H. "Rath City." *West Texas Historical Association Year Book* 24 (1948).

Koch, Lena Clara. "The Federal Indian Policy in Texas, 1845-1860." *Southwestern Historical Quarterly* 28 (January, April 1925).

Neighbours, Kenneth F. "Elm Creek Raid in Young County, 1864." *West Texas Historical Association Year Book* 40 (1964).

_____. "Tonkawa Scouts and Guides." *West Texas Historical Association Year Book* 49 (1973).

Pool, William C. "The Battle of Dove Creek." *Southwestern Historical Quarterly* 53 (April 1950).

Richardson, Rupert N. "Some Details of the Southern Overland Mail." *Southwestern Historical Quarterly* 29 (July 1925).

_____. "Jim Shaw the Delaware." *West Texas Historical Association Year Book* 3 (1927).

Rister, C.C. "The Significance of the Destruction of the Buffalo in the Southwest." *Southwestern Historical Quarterly* 33 (July 1929).

Roberts, Wilma Pinkston. "80 John Wallace: Black Rancher Who Died Wealthy." *Oeste* (December 1975).

Scholes, F.V., and H.P. Mera. "Some Aspects of the Jumano Problem." *Contributions to American Anthropology and History* 6 (1940).

Skaggs, Jimmy M. "John Thomas Lytle." *Southwestern Historical Quarterly* 71 (July 1967).

_____. "Northward Across the Plains: The Western Cattle Trail." *Great Plains Journal* 12 (Fall 1972).

_____. "The Route of the Great Western (Dodge City) Cattle Trail." *West Texas Historical Association Year Book* 41 (1965).

Smith, Ralph A. "The West Texas Bone Business." *West Texas Historical Association Year Book* 55 (1979).

Temple, Frank M. "Colonel B.H. Grierson's Administration of the District of the Pecos," *West Texas Historical Association Year Book* 38 (1962).

Tunnell, Curtis D. "Texas Heritage Lost: The Fate of Rath City." *Medallion* (October 1982).

Williams, J.W. "The Butterfield Overland Mail Road across Texas." *Southwestern Historical Quarterly* 61 (July 1957).

Index